St. Catharines Ontario Book 4 in Colour Photos, Saving Our History One Photo at a Time

Photography
by Barbara Raué
2018

Series Name:
Cruising Ontario

Book 192: St. Catharines Book 4

Cover photo: 183 King Street, Page 30

Series Name: Cruising Ontario
Saving Our History One Photo at a Time
in colour photos

Books Available in Alphabetical Order:
Aberfoyle, Acton, Alton, Amherstburg, Ancaster, Arthur, Aylmer, Ayr, Bloomingdale, Brantford, Burlington, Caledon, Caledonia, Cambridge, Clifford, Conestogo, Delhi, Dorchester to Aylmer, Drayton, Drumbo, Dundas, Eden Mills, Elmira, Elora, Essex, Fergus, Guelph, Hagersville, Hamilton, Hanover, Harriston, Hespeler, Jarvis, Kingston, Kingsville, Kitchener, Linwood, Listowel, London, Lucknow, Mono, Mount Forest, Neustadt, New Hamburg, Niagara-on-the-Lake, Oakville, Orangeville, Orillia, Owen Sound, Palmerston, Peterborough, Petrolia, Port Elgin, Preston, Rockwood, Sarnia, Seaforth, Sheffield, Shelburne, Simcoe, Southampton, St. Jacobs, St. Marys, St. Thomas, Stoney Creek, Stratford, Thamesford, Tillsonburg, Waterdown, Waterford, Waterloo, Welland, Wellesley, Windsor, Wingham, Woodstock

Book 157: Brockville
Book 158: Merrickville
Book 159: Smiths Falls
Book 160: Portland, Newboro
Book 161: Westport & Area
Book 162: Perth
Book 163-166: Belleville
Book 167-168: Port Colborne
Book 169: Erin in Colour
Book 170: Goderich in Colour
Book 171: Sault Ste. Marie
Book 172: Lake Superior
Book 173-176: Thunder Bay
Book 177-179: Paris

Book 180: St. George
Book 182-183: Burford
Book 184: Mt Pleasant, Onondaga, Newport
Book 185-186: Grimsby
Book 187: Toronto in Colour
Book 188: Collingwood Colour
Book 189-193: St. Catharines

Other Books by Barbara Raue

Coins of Gold

Arrows, Indians and Love

The Life and Times of Barbara
Volume 1: Inventions That Have Enhanced My Life
Volume 2: Entertainment That I Have Enjoyed
Volume 3: East Coast Trips
Volume 4: Olympics Have Always Intrigued Me
Volume 5: Wonders of the World
Volume 6: Caribbean Cruises We Have Enjoyed
Volume 7: Animals
Volume 8: Storms and Other Major Disasters in My Lifetime
Volume 9: Wars, Terrorist Attacks and Major Disasters

The Cromwell Family Book

Laura Secord Discovered

Daddy Where Are You?

Montana Series
Book 1: Montana Dream
Book 2: Life on the Montana Frontier
Book 3: Montana to Boston and Back
Book 4: Montana Sons Go to War
Book 5: Montana Sons Return From War

Visit Barbara's website to view all of her books
http://barbararaue.ca

Table of Contents

Church Street	Page 6
James Street	Page 20
King Street	Page 24
Lake Street	Page 33
Midland Street	Page 41
Montebello Place	Page 42
Norris Place	Page 50
Ontario Street	Page 53
Geneva Street	Page 58
Architectural Terms	Page 60
Building Styles	Page 65

Before this area was settled several Indian trails intersected here at a ford in Twelve Mile Creek. They were improved by early settlers and a church was erected at the crossroads by 1798. A tavern soon followed and a settlement began to grow. After the War of 1812, the community expanded largely through the efforts of William Hamilton Merritt. He was the chief promoter of the first Welland Canal built in 1824-33. The canal made St. Catharines a centre for water transportation, and provided abundant water power for industry. Factories and mills were established and St. Catharines became a leading flour-milling and shipbuilding centre.

Dr. Lucius Oille was born in 1830 and was one of St. Catharines most prominent citizens. He served as a member of council for several years before becoming mayor in 1878. He was the second mayor of the city and first chairman of the waterworks. Oille was a physician and owned the first x-ray machine in St. Catharine. He was involved in dozens of city projects, such as the organization of the Niagara Central Railway and the city's first streetcar system. In 1878 Dr. Oille donated a fountain in front of the courthouse at the corner of King and James Street to the citizens of St. Catharines. He wanted to provide water to citizens who were shopping in the market square or had come downtown to work. Tin drinking cups were attached to the fountain by a chain so that people could use them to drink. Dr. Oille even thought of the animals as the fountain has a small basin at the bottom specifically for them. This gift marked the establishment of the city's waterworks system in 1875-1876. Dr. Lucius Oille died on August 15, 1903.

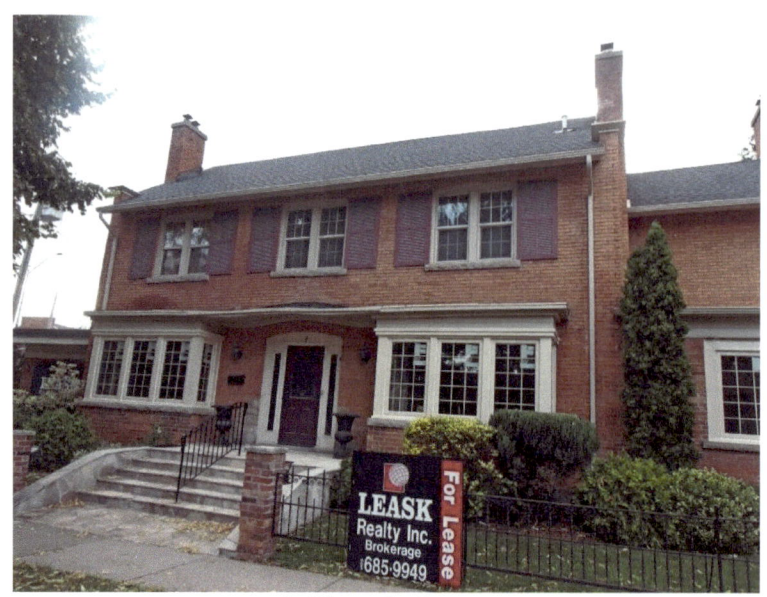
1 Church Street

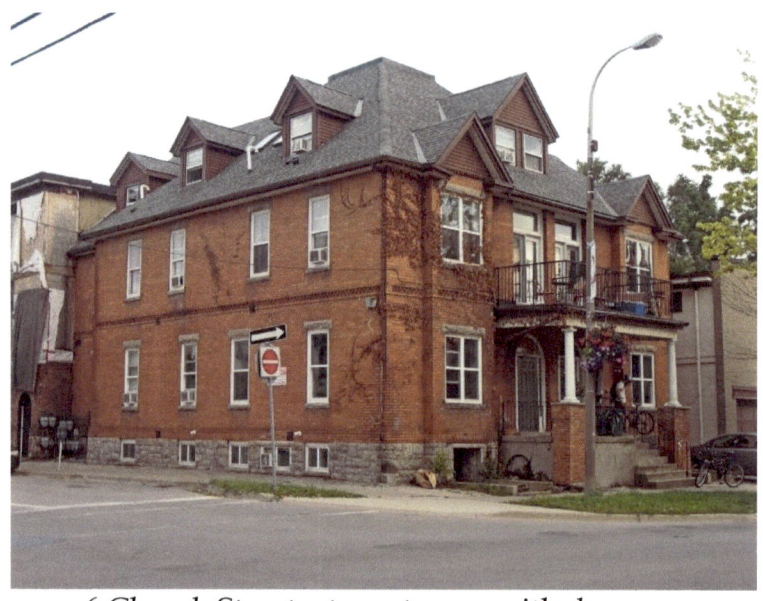
6 Church Street – two storeys with dormers

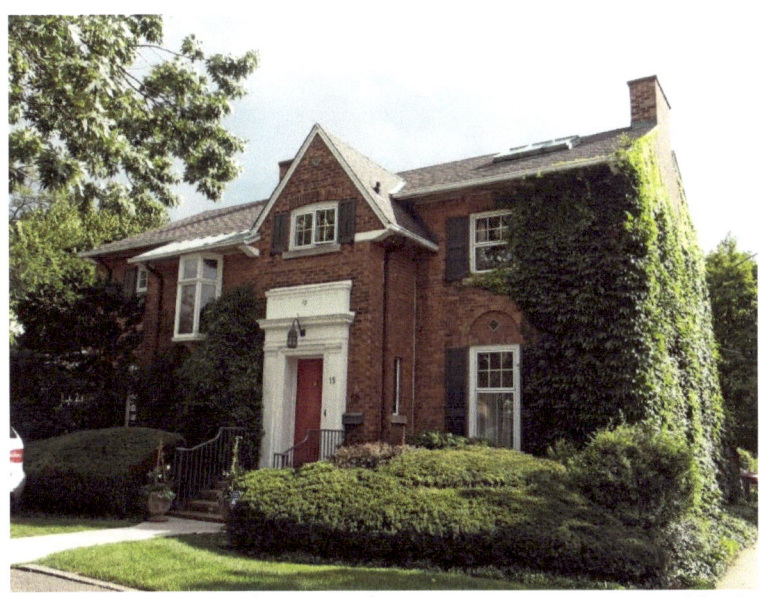

15 Church Street - 1½ storey frontispiece entrance – Heritage Building

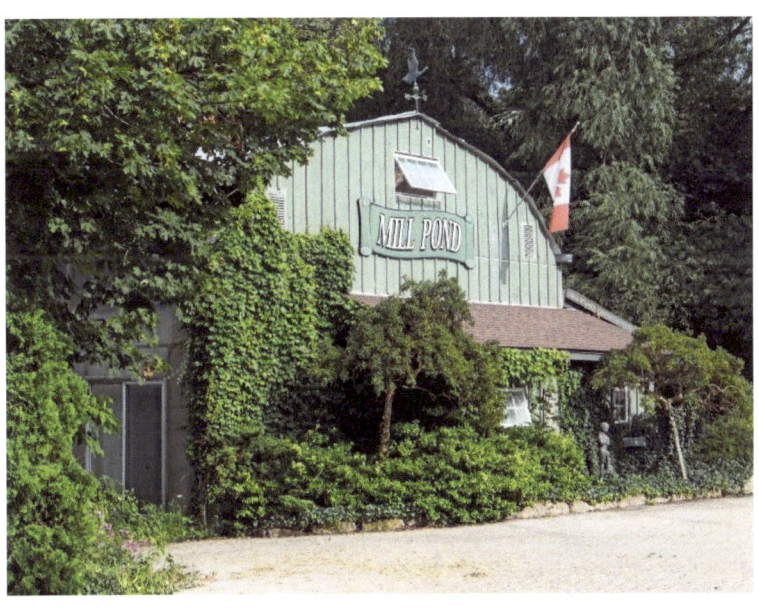

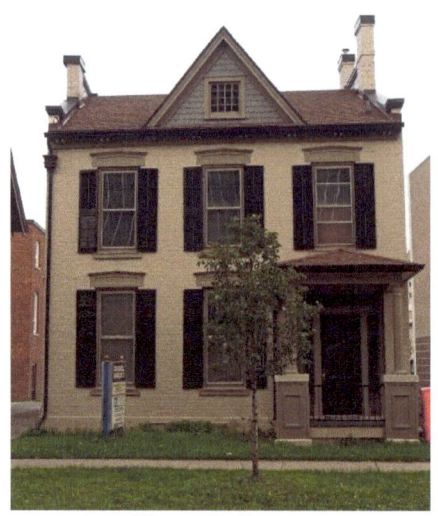

Church Street

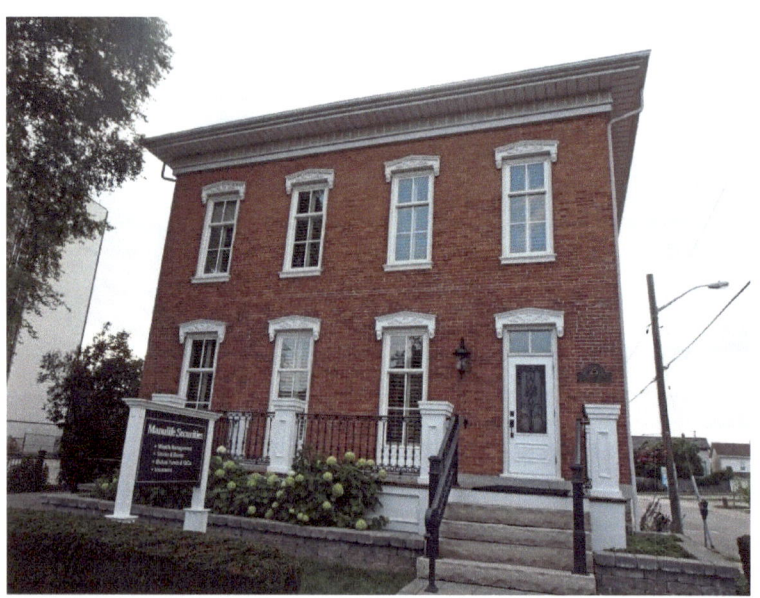

25 Church Street – decorative window hoods

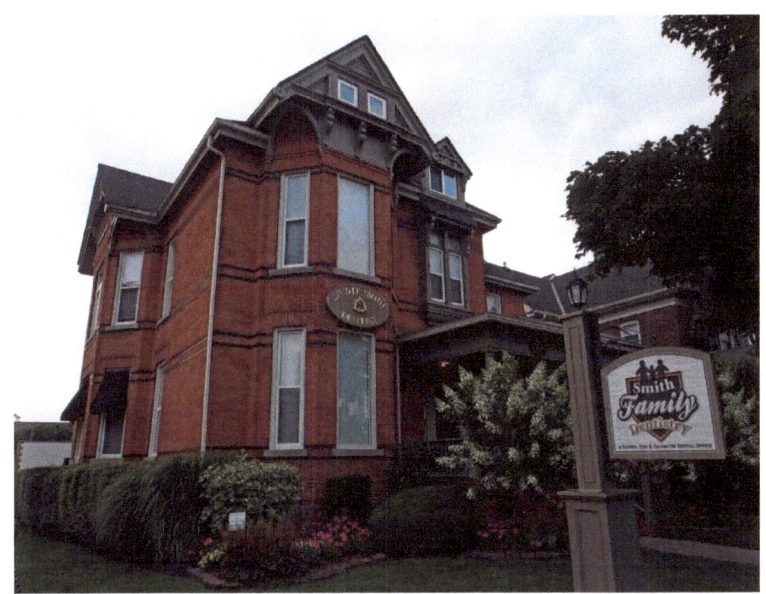

27 Church Street – Italianate – 2½ storey bay windows, fretwork, dormer

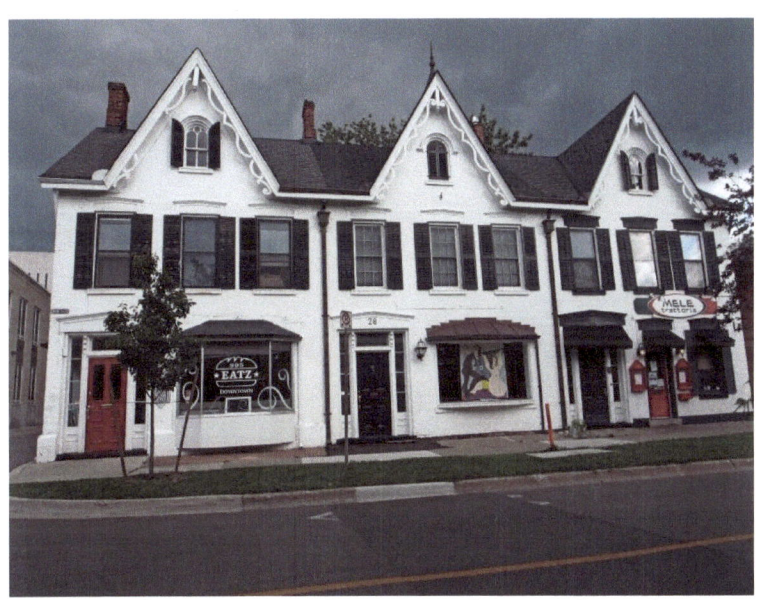

26-30 Church Street – Gothic Revival, verge board trim and finials on gables

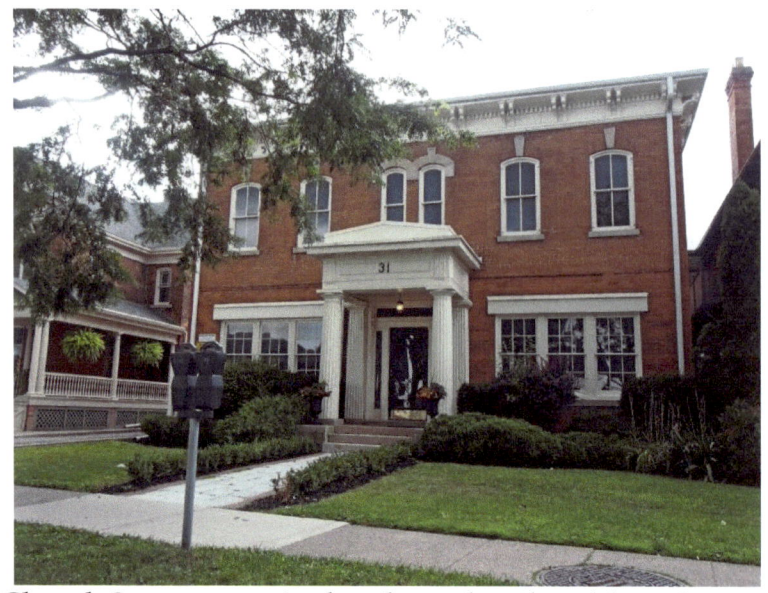

31 Church Street – cornice brackets, dentil molding, keystones and voussoirs, free standing and engaged columns, sidelights and transom windows around door

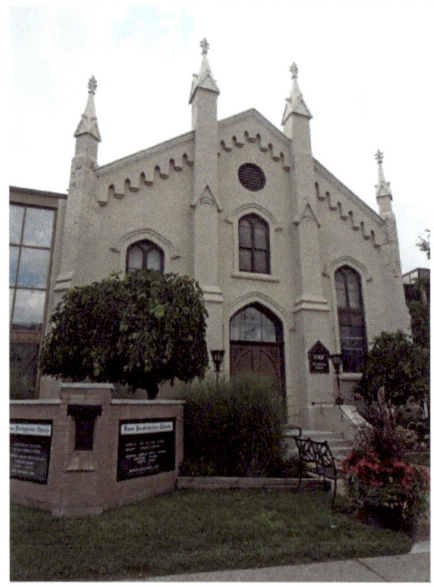

53 Church Street – Knox Presbyterian Church – Gothic – dentil molding, buttresses with finials, lancet windows

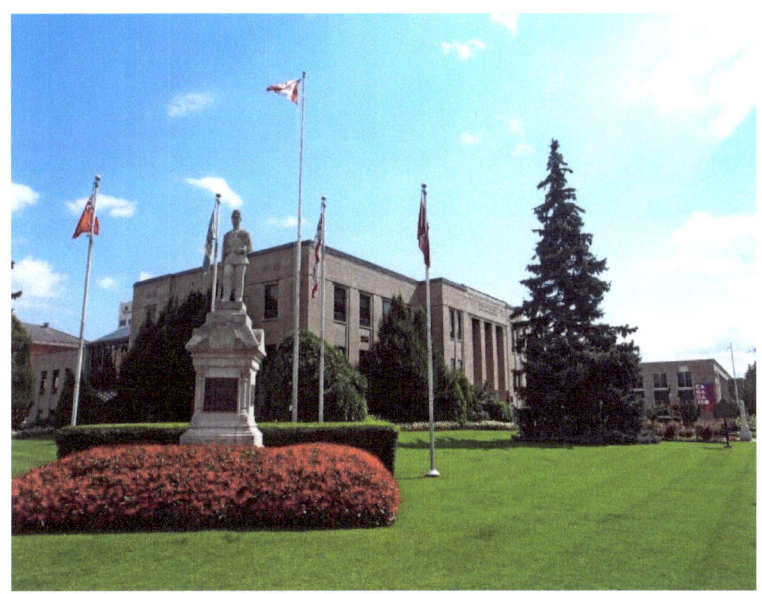

50 Church Street – City Hall built in 1937 is a two-storey Queenston limestone with a basement and partial sub-basement. The roof is flat with a raised pediment above the doorway and a parapet extending around the remainder of the building. There are three pairs of glazed brass doors recessed behind massive pilasters extending the second floor ceiling. Three storey-high glass windows light the main stairway. Decorative panels extend around the exterior walls just below the roof line.

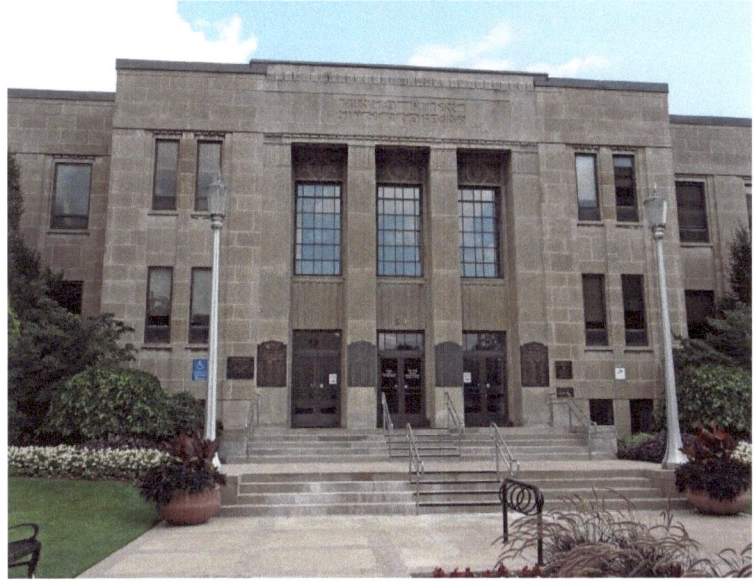

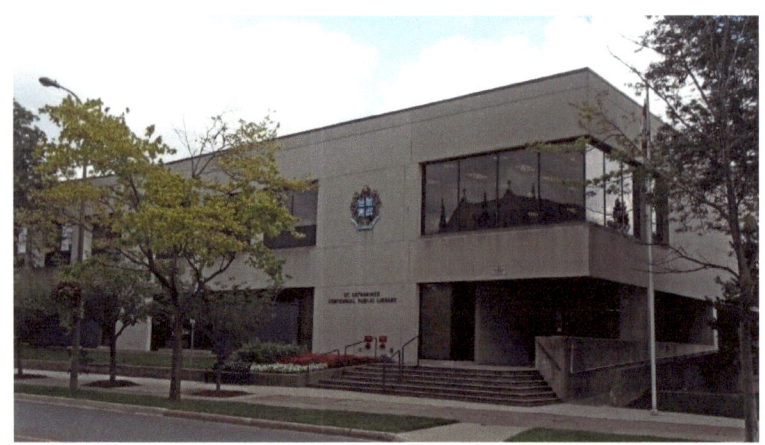
54 Church Street – St. Catharines Central Public Library

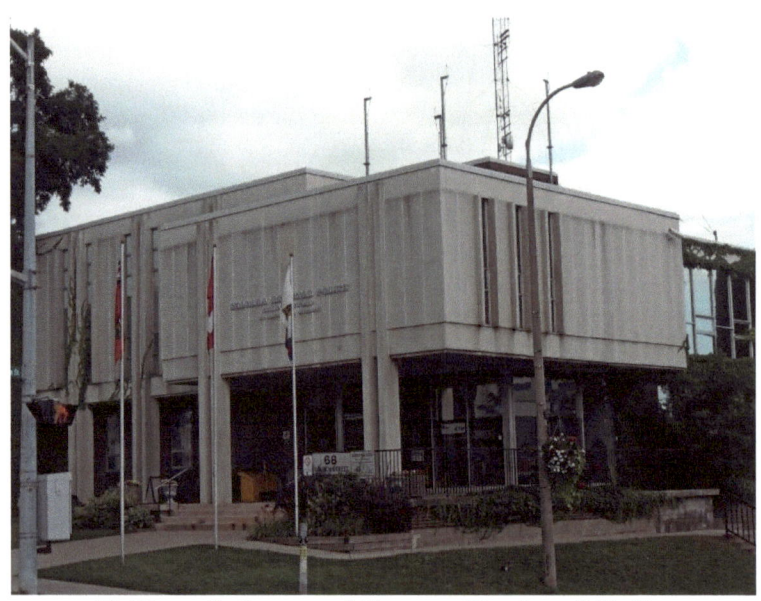
68 Church Street – Niagara Regional Police

Like many growing communities in the 1800s and 1900s, religion played a major role in the everyday life of its citizens. A number of churches were built in St. Catharines providing services in a variety of denominations.

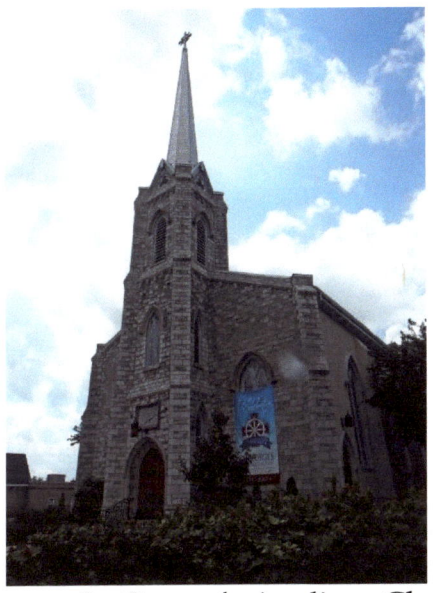

83 Church Street – St. George's Anglican Church took five years to build and it opened in 1840.

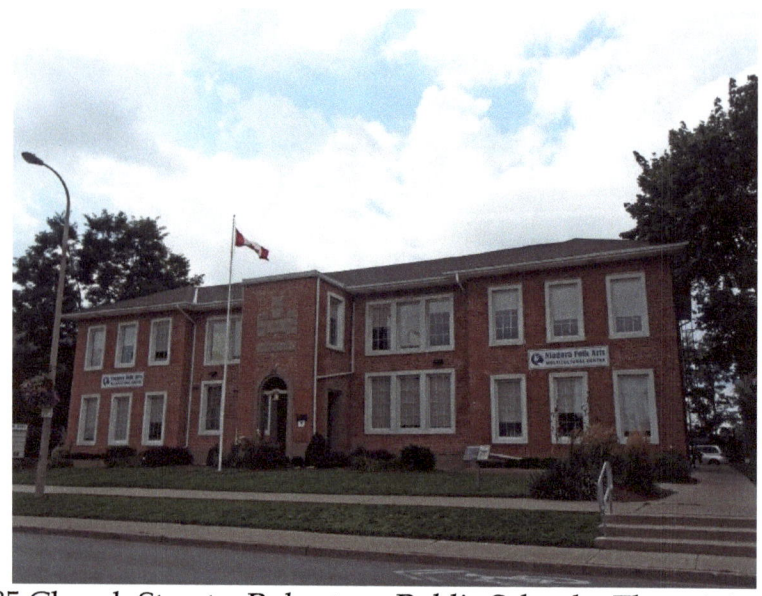

85 Church Street – Robertson Public School – The original section as constructed in 1829. The roof is a medium hip with two additional hips as either end. The windows are two-sash, double-hung with six panes of glass in each section. The portico has a bell dating to the 1820s, and a large date stone.

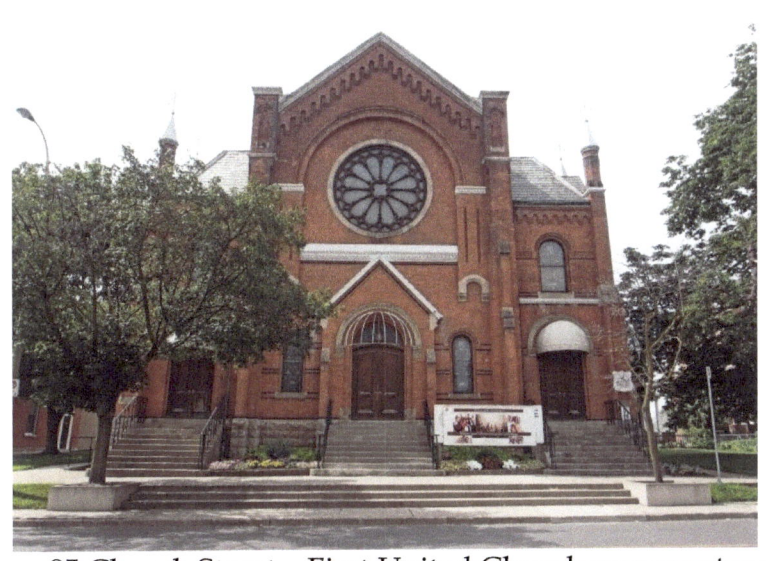

95 Church Street – First United Church was constructed in 1877 in the Lombard Romanesque style of architecture which is characterized by a gable roof across the front of the church and a projecting entrance. It has rounded arches for doors and window openings. Four detailed buttresses rise up as towers, each supporting a small metal spire. The twelve petal stained glass rose window is a prominent feature on the front façade.

It is now known as Royal House Redeemed Christian Church of God.

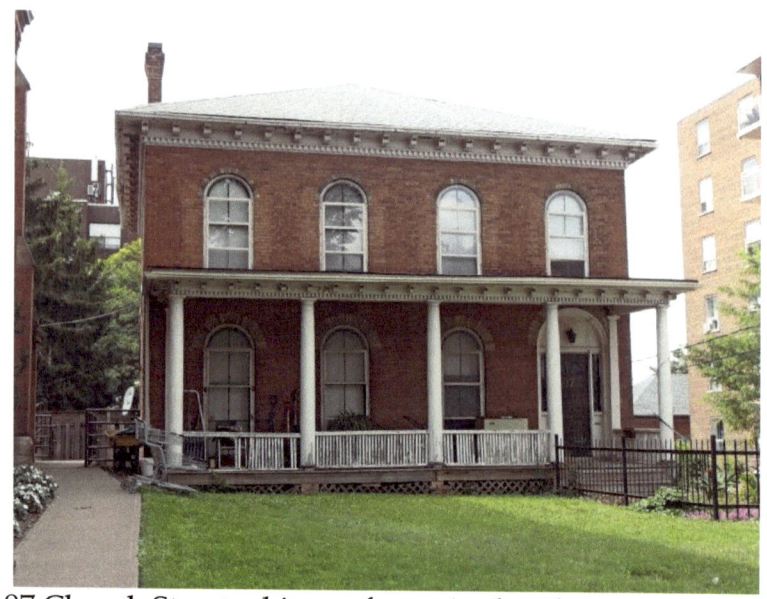

97 Church Street – hip roof, cornice brackets with dentil molding, voussoirs over windows and door, sidelights

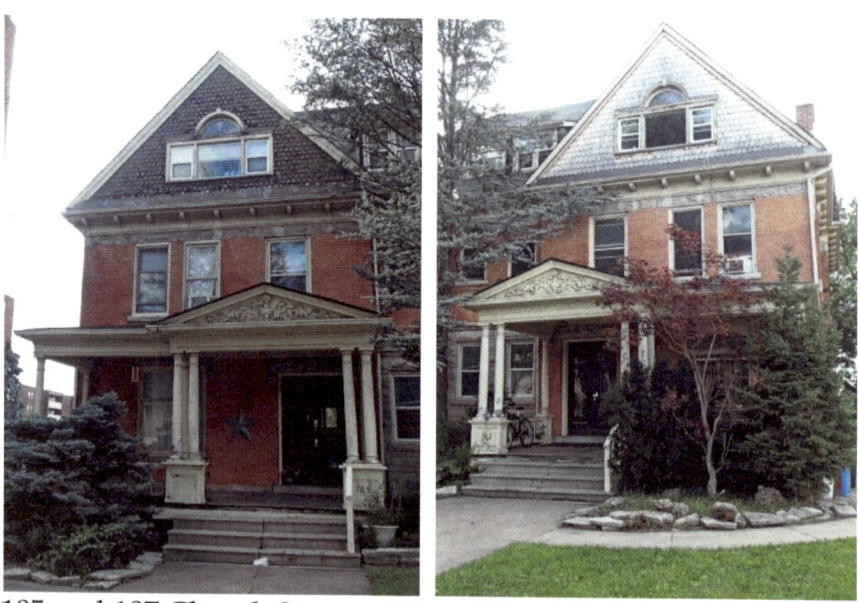

105 and 107 Church Street – Edwardian – Palladian window in gable, pediment with decorated tympanum

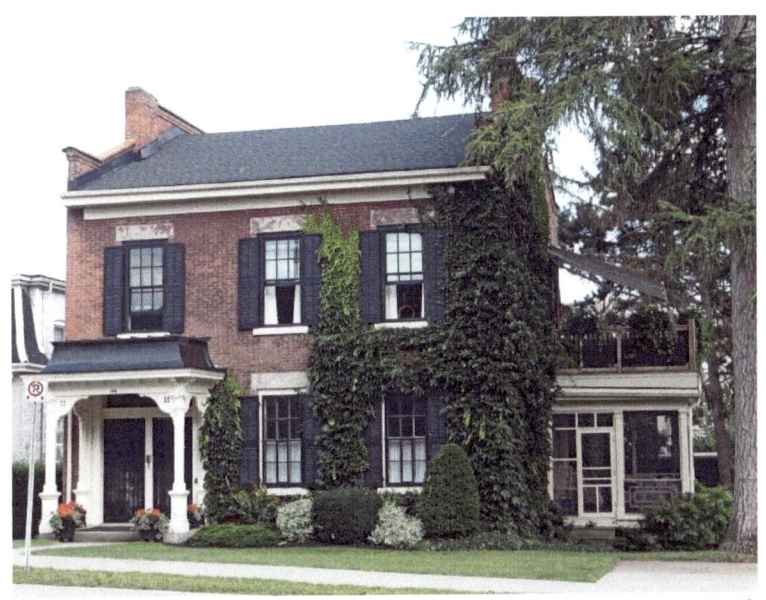

104 Church Street – decorative entrance, shutters on windows

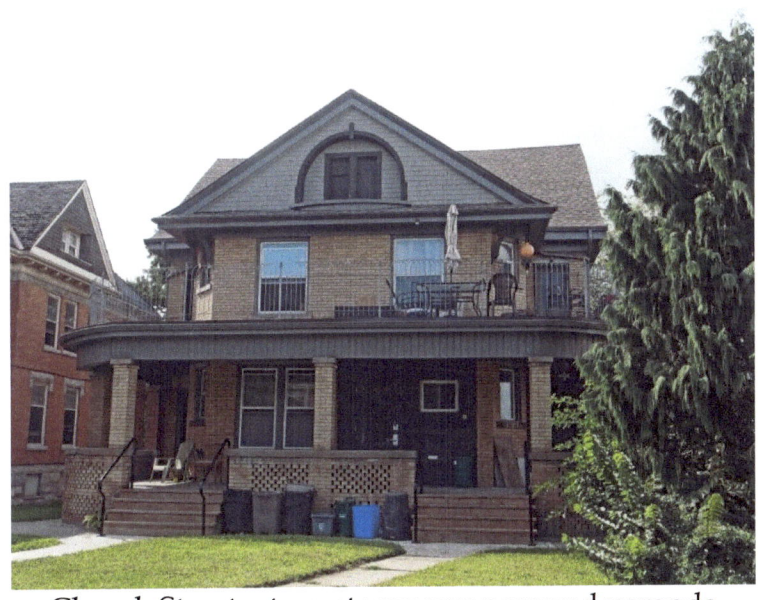

Church Street – two-storey wraparound veranda

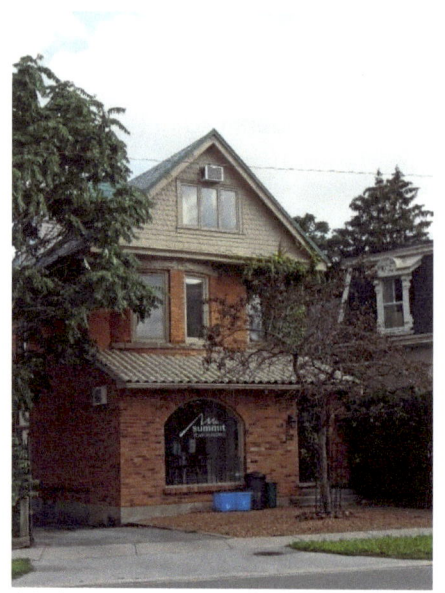

108½ Church Street - Edwardian

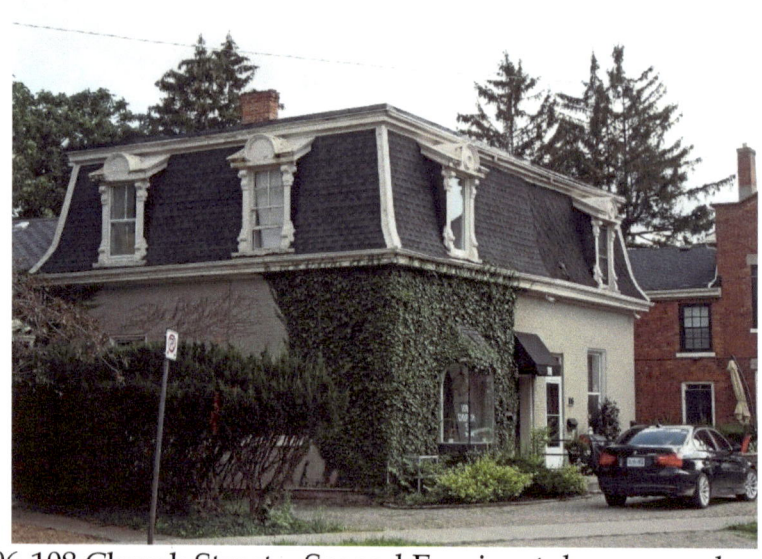

106-108 Church Street – Second Empire style, mansard roof, dormers with window hoods

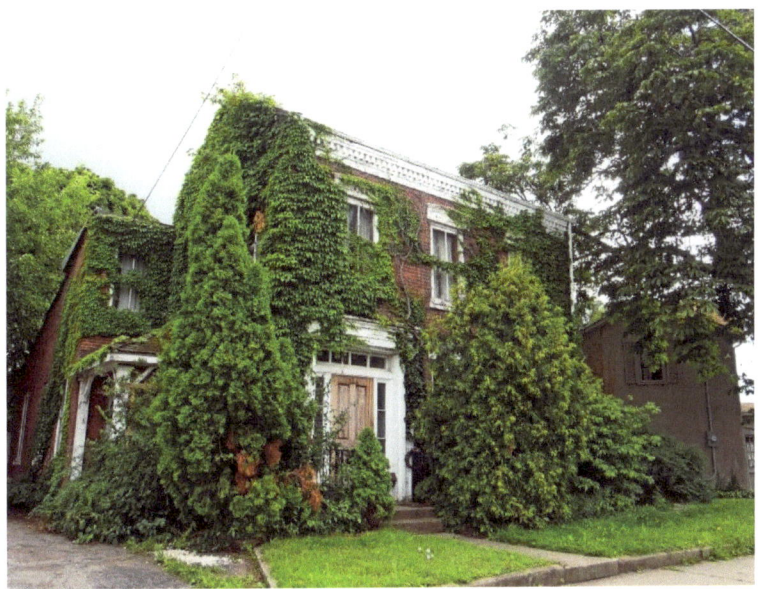

134 Church Street – Wood-Grantham-Bacher House c. 1852 – It is a two storey dwelling of red brick with a medium gable roof trimmed with a decorative frieze in contrasting brick. There are sidelights and transom windows around door.

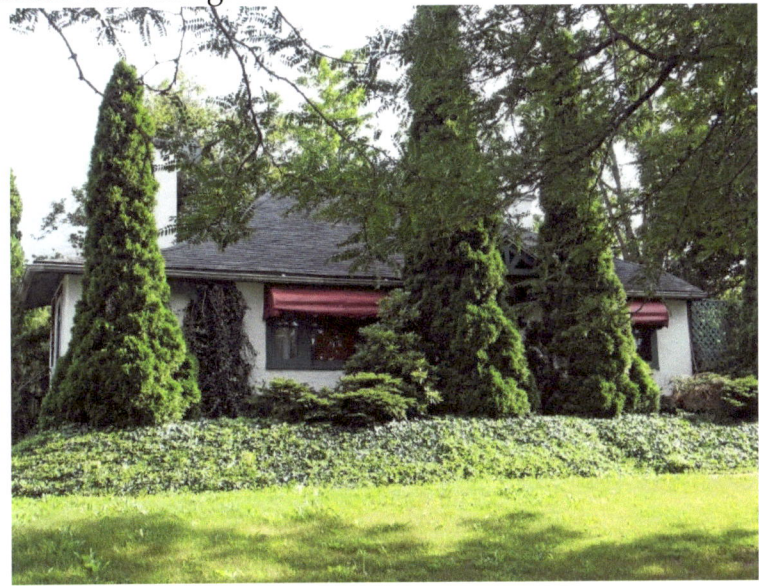

Church Street

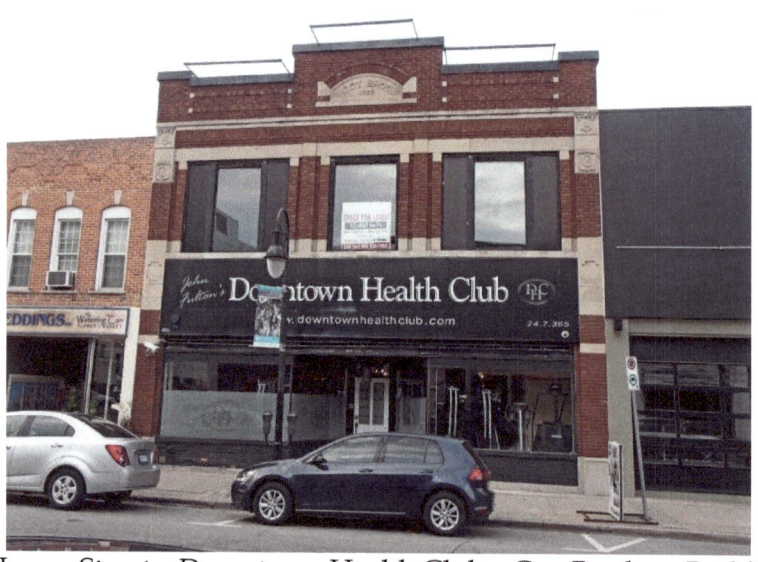

14 James Street – Downtown Health Club – Coy Brothers Building 1922 – stepped parapet, pilasters with decorative blocks

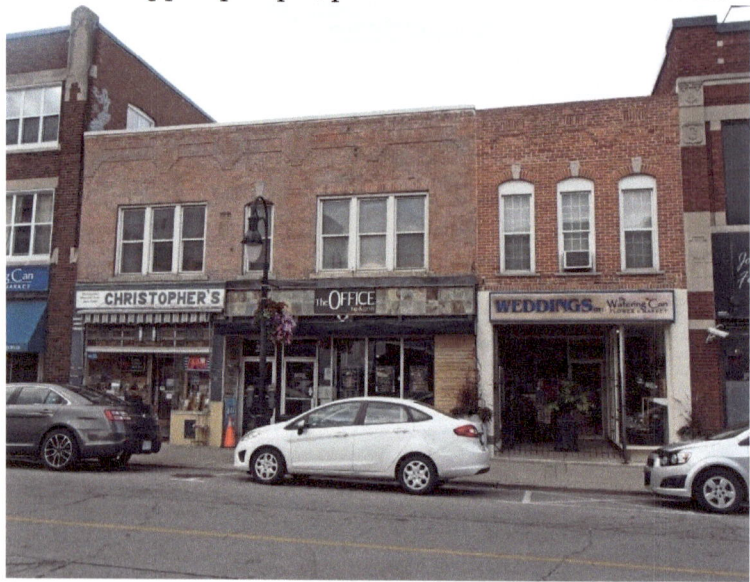

26 James Street – Christopher's Variety Store – decorative brickwork, voussoirs and keystones above the windows of The Watering Can Flower Market

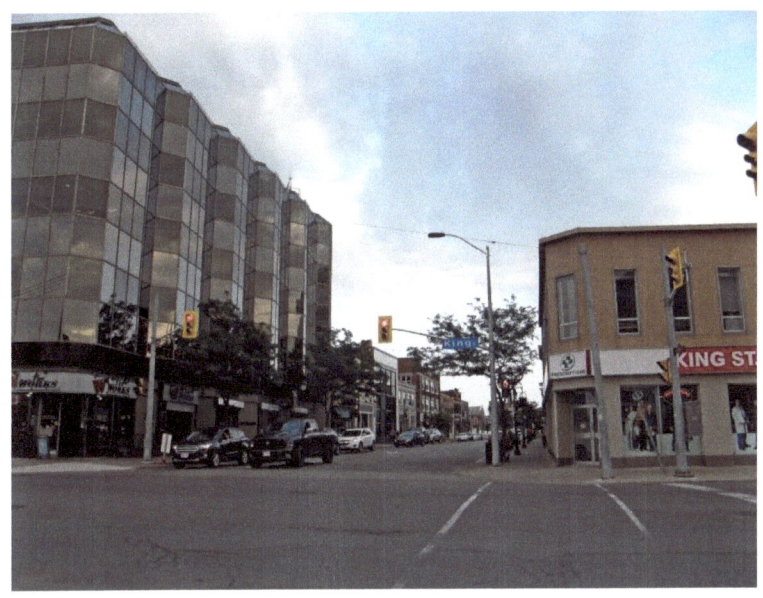

James Street

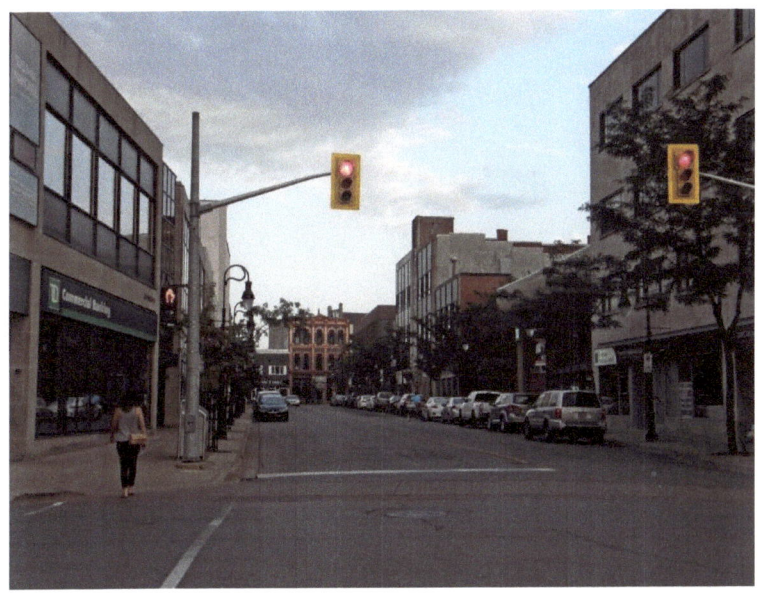

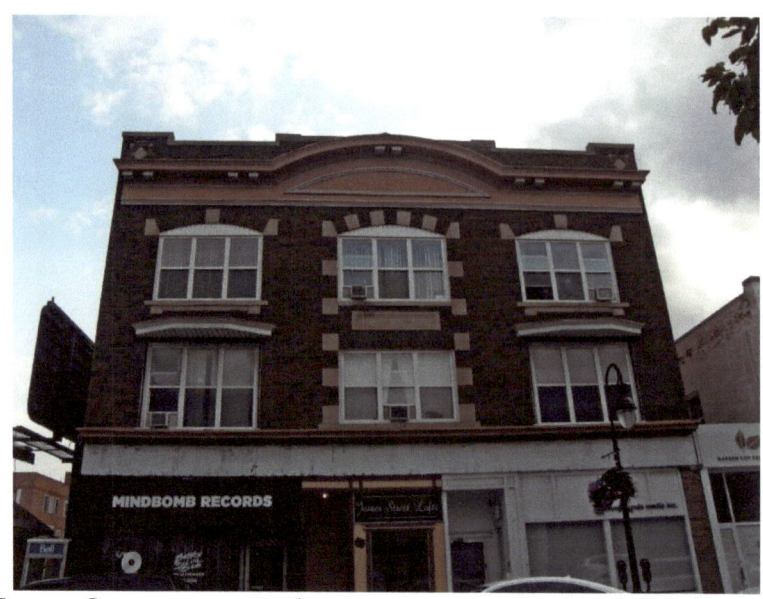

27 James Street – stepped parapet, two-tone brickwork around windows

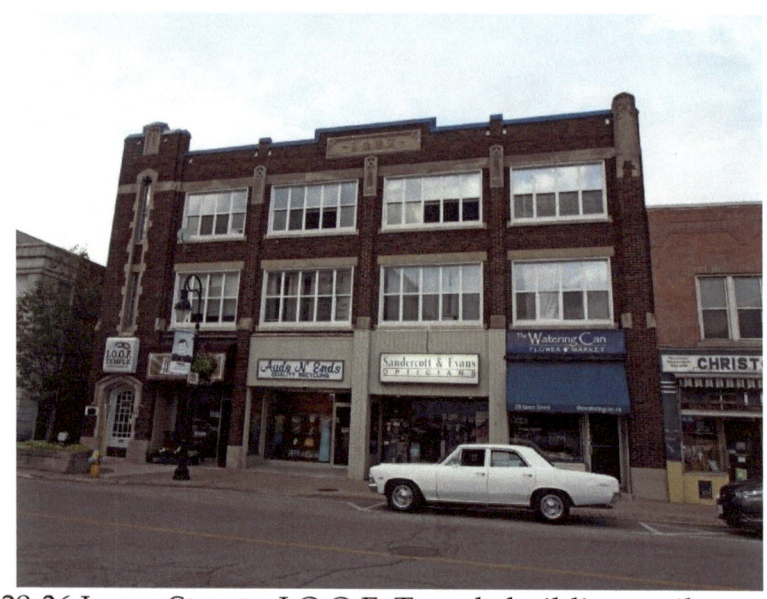

28-36 James Street – I.O.O.F. Temple building – pilasters, banding, stepped parapet

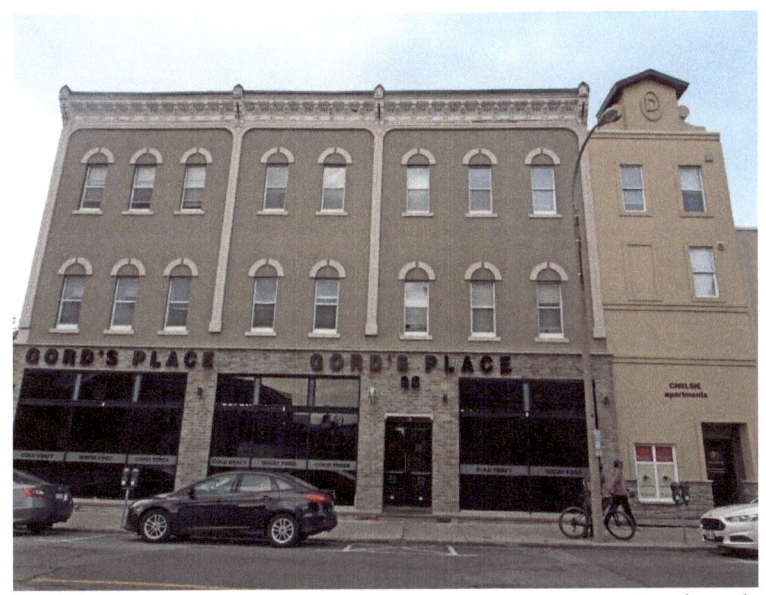

84 James Street – Gord's Place Restaurant – cornice brackets and decorative cornice

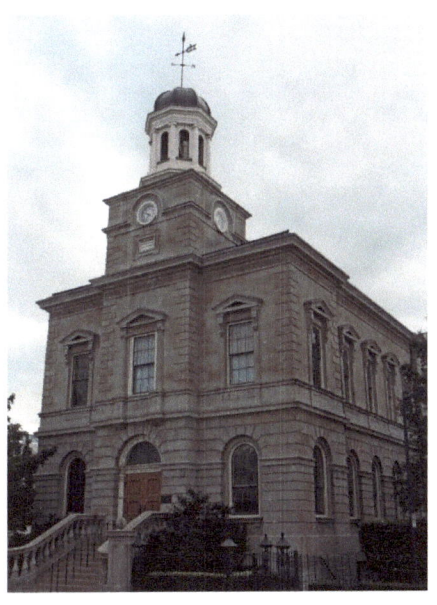

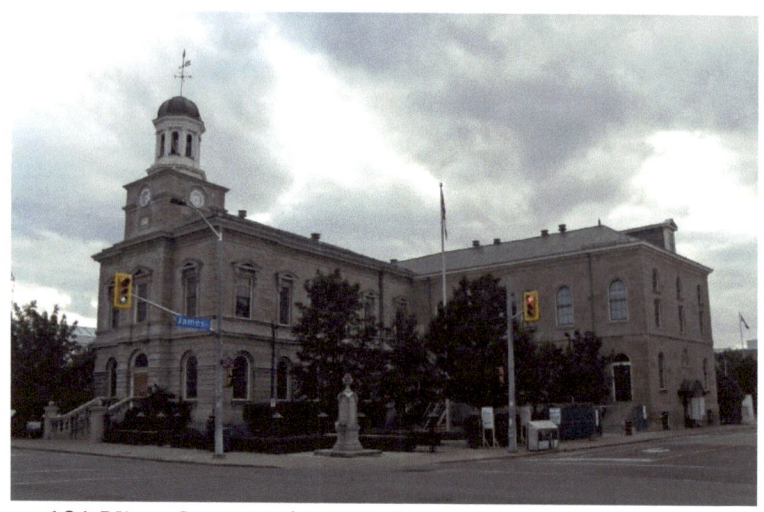

101 King Street – former Court House – Georgian style – 1848-1849 – The visible James and King Street facades are of channelled Queenston ashlars while the concealed west and north walls are constructed with a course rubble limestone and brick, respectively. The front façade has a tower with a three-faced striking clock and is topped by an octagonal cupola. The clock continues to chime with the assistance of the original weights which extend from the clock tower to the first floor. The entrance to the building is carved in stone like the town hall in Perugia, Italy. It features upright balustrades which conform to the slope of the stairway. The supporting columns under the copings on each side are individually carved to fit its specific location. The northeast wing cut-stone addition to the original structure was built in 1865 to accommodate the County offices and courthouse.

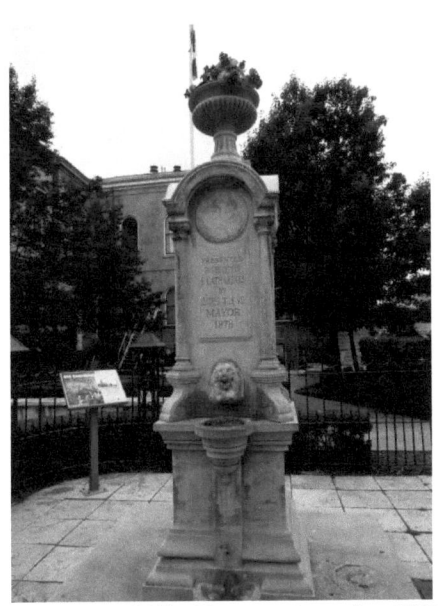

101 King Street – Oille Fountain – In 1878 the Mayor of St. Catharines, Dr. Lucius S. Oille, donated three horse watering troughs and a fountain to the City. They marked the opening of the City's waterworks system. It is an eight feet tall, two feet squared carved-stone monument in the Classical style. Around the base is a plinth housing a semi-circular drinking basin for pets and surmounted by a rectangular base two feet tall topped by a narrow belt course. At this height, two projecting stone fountain bowls occupy opposite sides. Both bowls are fed by carved lions' heads with water emerging from the mouths; patrons drank from tin cups suspended from chains. Above this height the fountain has corner pilasters supporting intersecting molded arches forming the top of the monument. The fountain is topped with a stone flower urn specifically designated by the donor for geraniums to be planted.

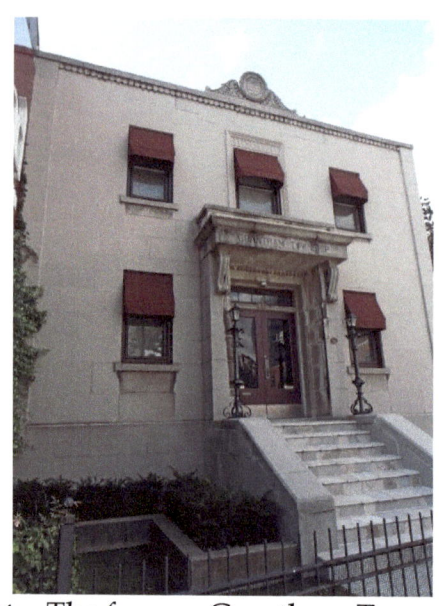

145 King Street – The former Grantham Town Hall was built in 1950 in the Contemporary International style with some Art Deco features. The Grantham crest over the center bay, frieze, window frames, and portico are all of stone.

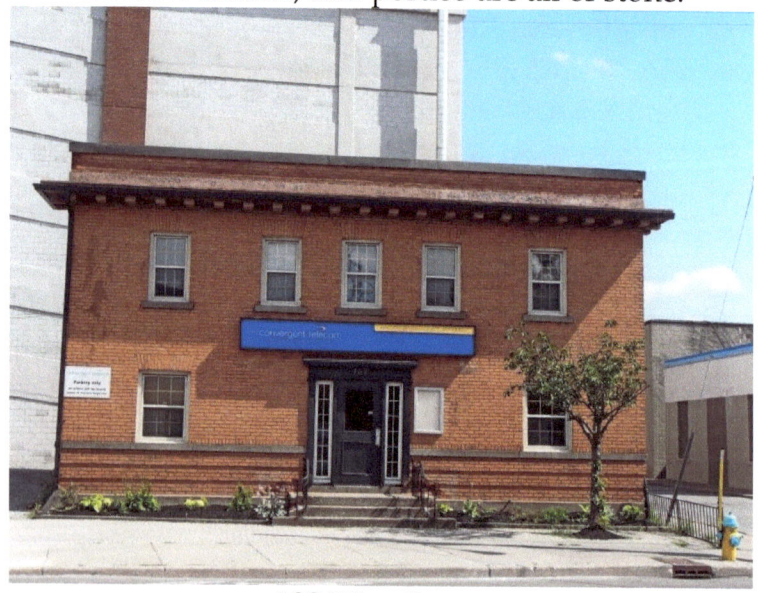

132 King Street

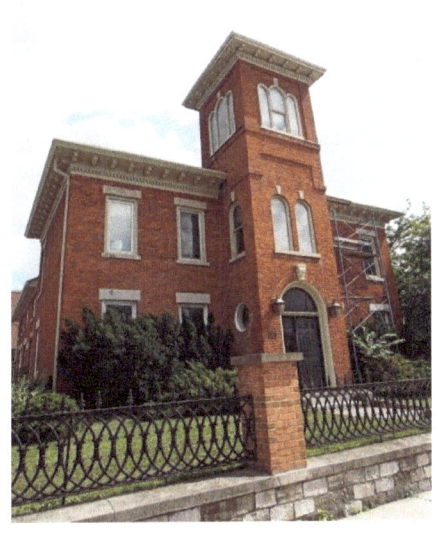

164 King Street – three storey tower with voussoirs and keystones; cornice brackets

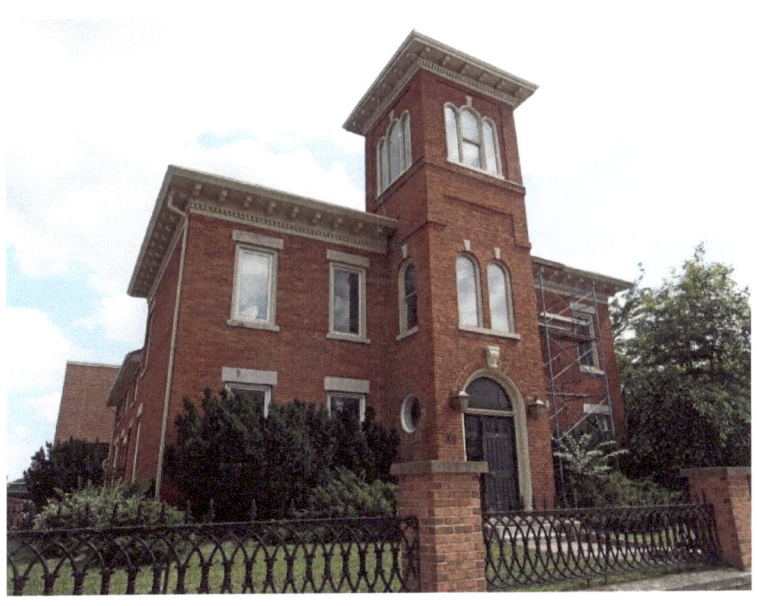

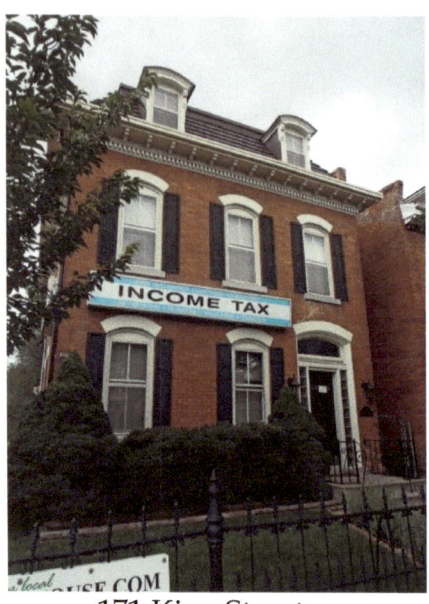
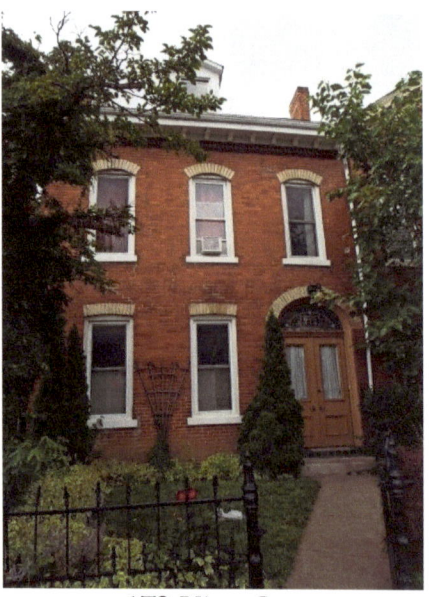

171 King Street
Dormers, brackets, dentil molding

173 King Street
voussoirs, transom

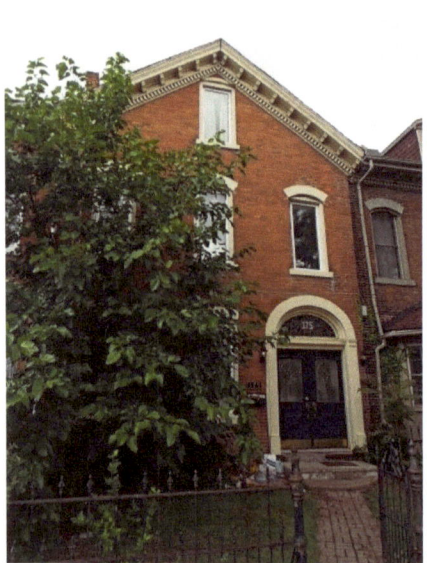
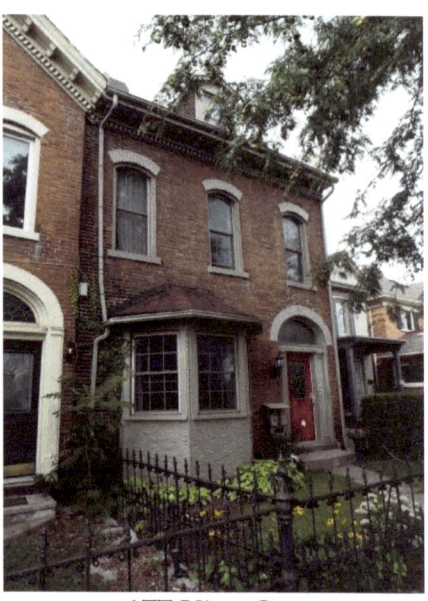

175 King Street
Brackets in gable, transom

177 King Street
bay window, voussoirs

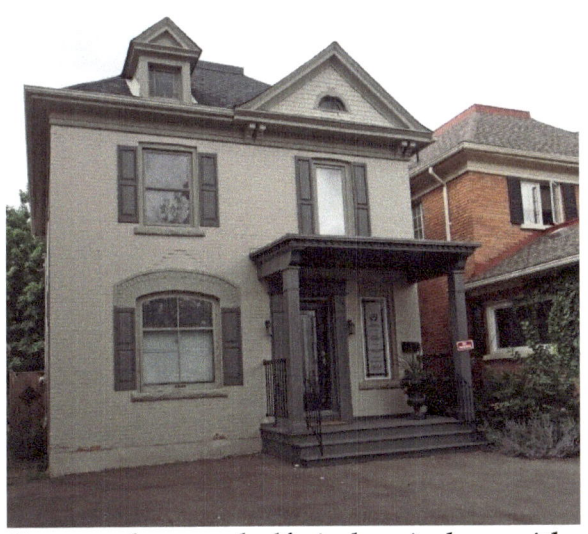

179 King Street – dormer, half-circle window with voussoirs and keystone in the gable which has fish scale patterning; paired cornice brackets and dentil molding below gable

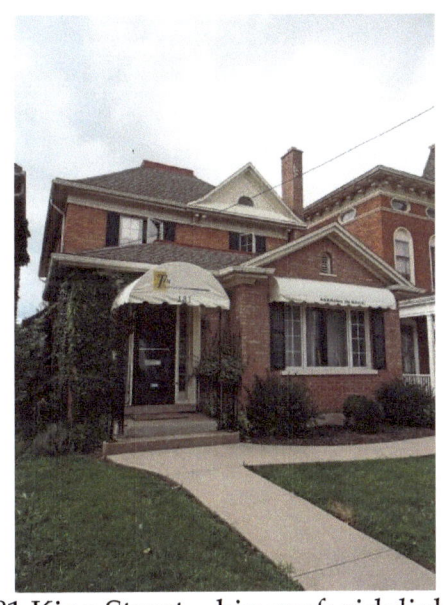

181 King Street – hip roof; sidelights

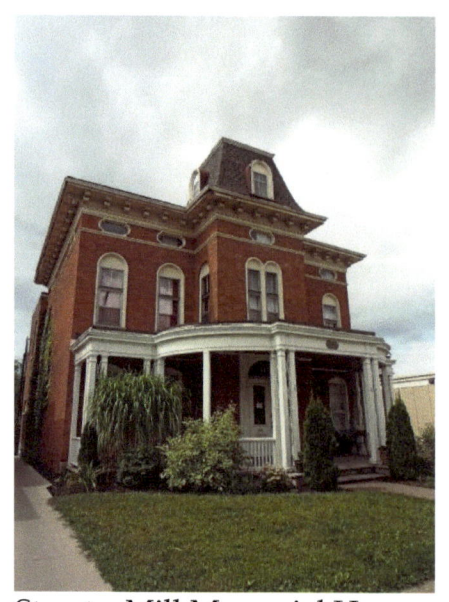

183 King Street – Mill Memorial Home was built in 1868 for James Mills, a founding member of the YMCA. The structure is a two and one half storey brick home built with Italianate design influences. It features a central tower and decorative roofline brackets. The tower has a mansard roof and semi-circular dormers. There are oval windows set between two courses of white brick which are located below the boxed cornice, decorative frieze and brackets of the roofline. The main floor windows are segmental with plain trim and a continuous stone sill. The upper windows are set in semi-circular frames. The main doorway has a fan transom and a panelled door. The large veranda, supported by sets of wooden columns, stretches across the entire front façade; it is a later addition to the house.

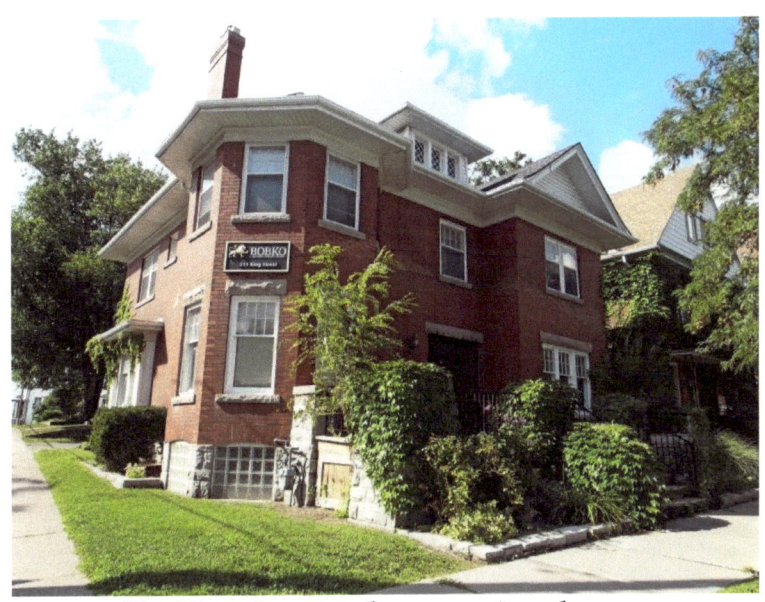

211 King Street – deep cornice, dormer

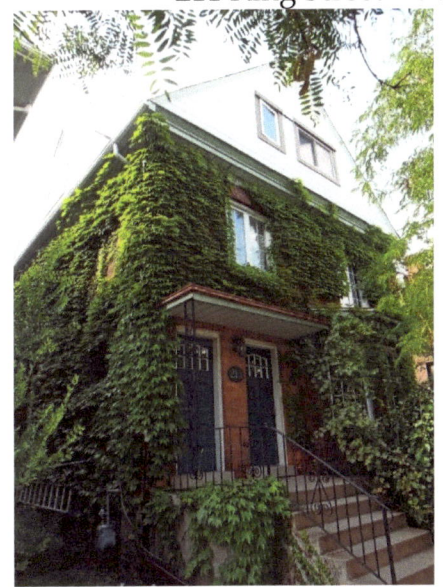

213 King Street

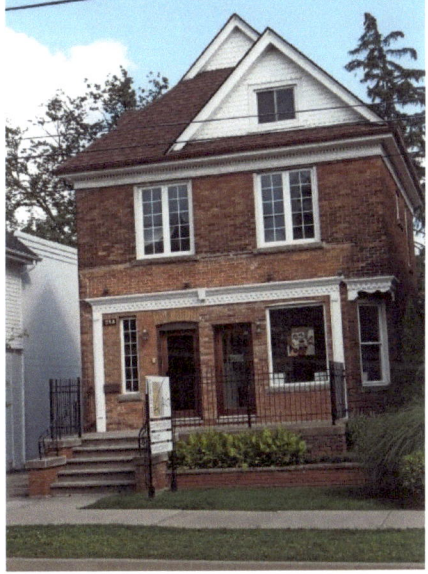

214 King Street
Fish scale patterning in gables
Hood above window at right

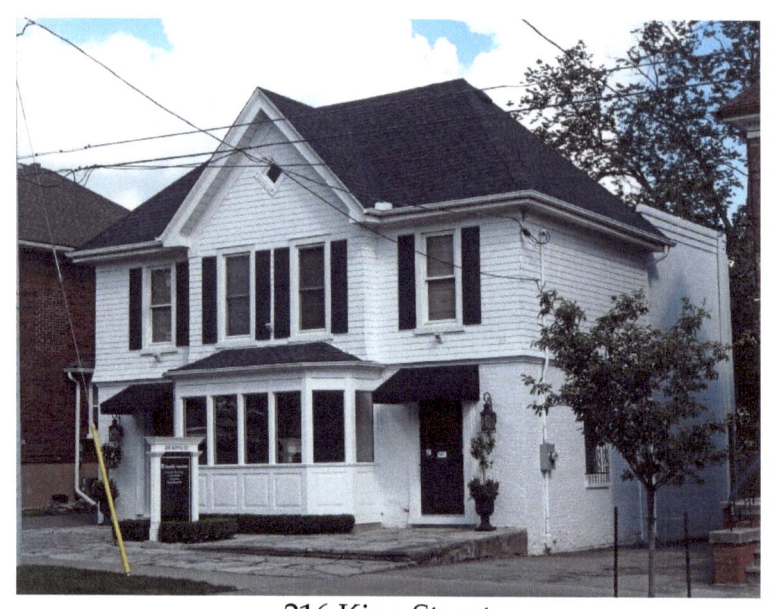

216 King Street

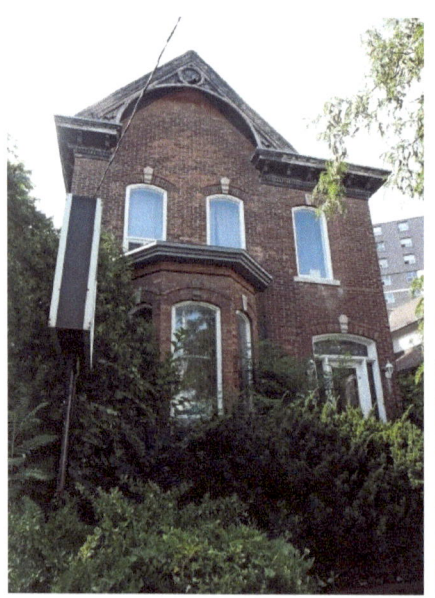

King Street
Verge board trim, bay window,
Voussoirs and keystones

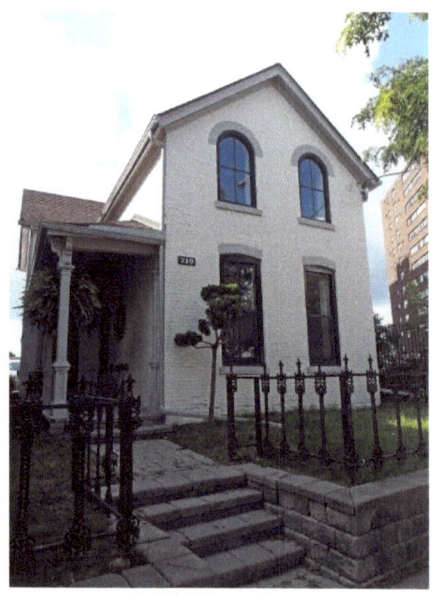

219 King Street

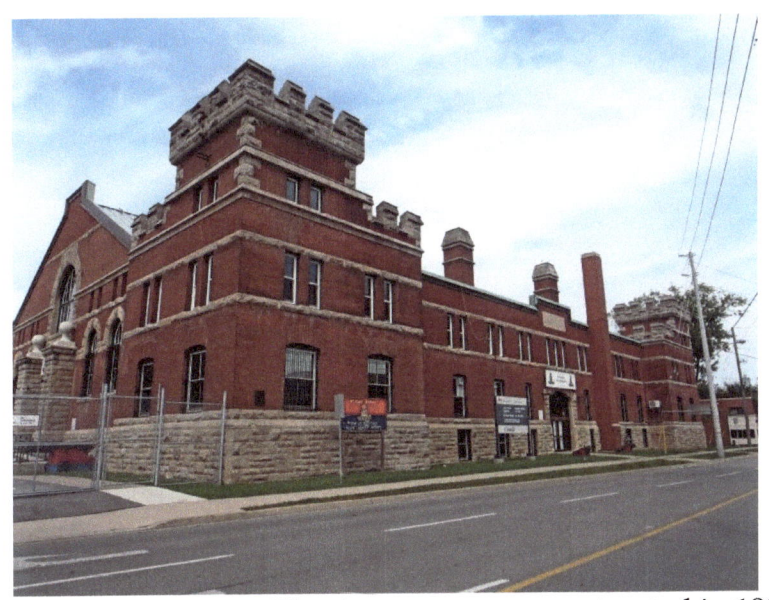

81 Lake Street – The Armoury was constructed in 1905 and was designed to serve as the regimental headquarters of the local militia and continues to function as a drill hall. It was from The Armoury that local militia units left to go overseas in 1914 and 1939, and for peacekeeping duties.

The bulky, rectangular shape of the armoury is relieved by an irregular roofline and the stylistic diversity of its two basic constituencies. The expansive gable roof and the rhythmic course of arched windows marking the drill hall contrast with the crenelated towers, jutting chimneys, and rigorous fenestration patterns of the street elevations. The use of consistent materials and continuous horizontal elements unifies the overall composition. Quarry faced stonework is juxtaposed with fields of flat brickwork which accentuate the visual links afforded by the massive foundations, string courses and copings. The interplay of colors and textures inherent on the masonry is an essential feature.

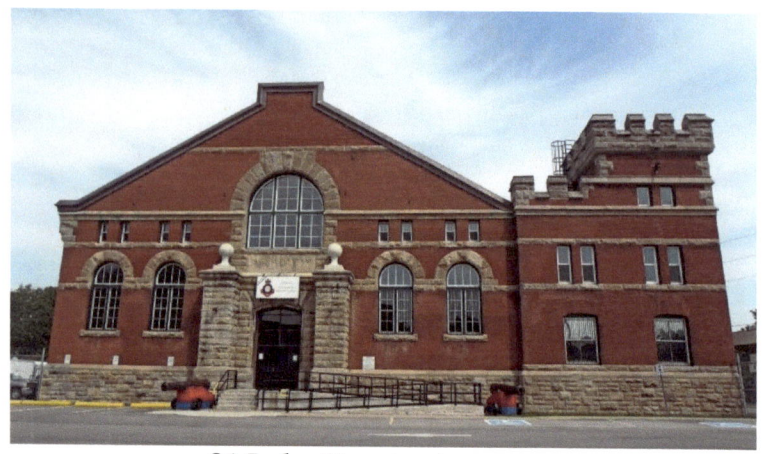

81 Lake Street - Armoury

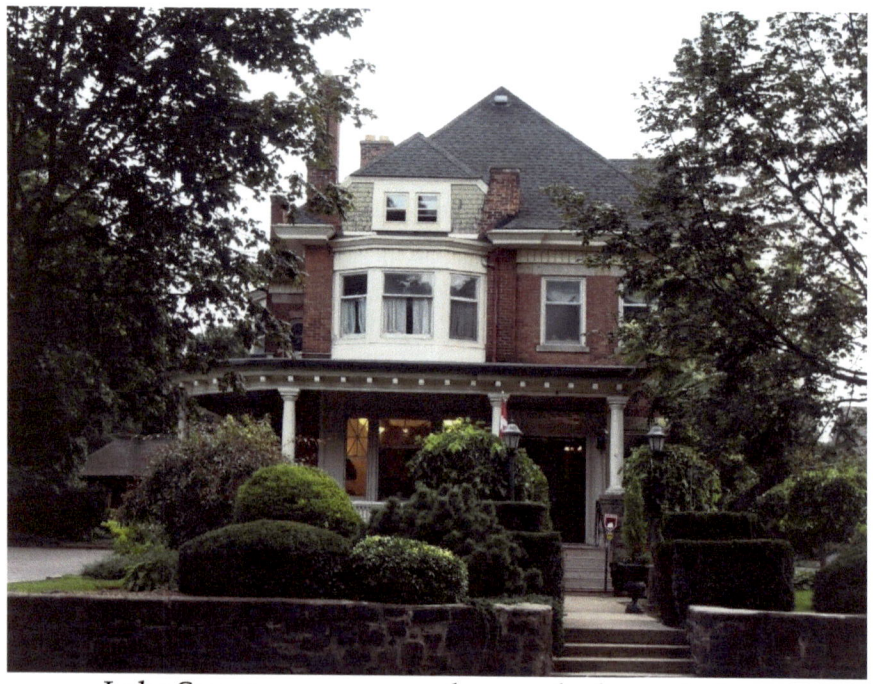

Lake Street – wraparound veranda, bay window

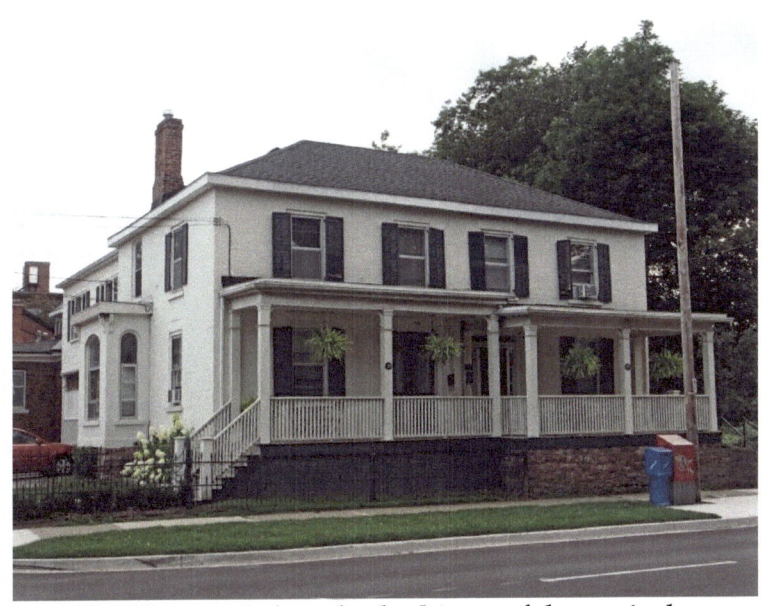

113-115 – semi-detached – hip roof, bay window

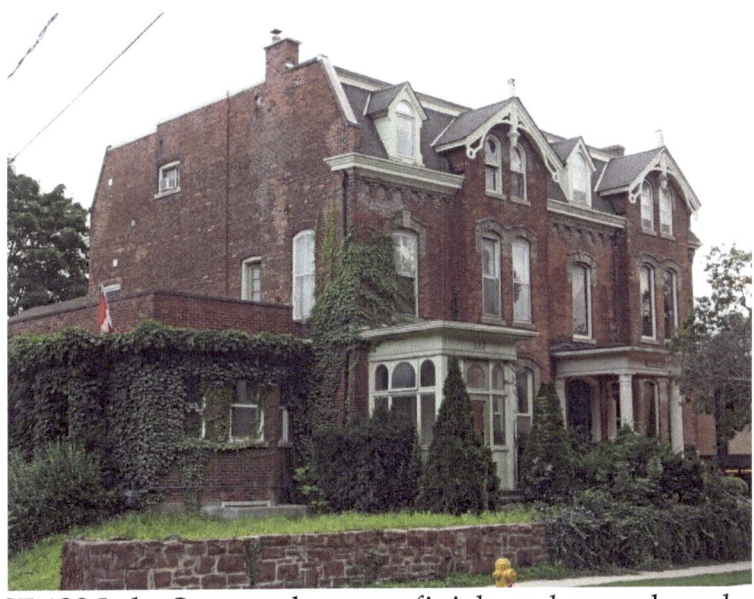

127-129 Lake Street – dormers, finials and verge board on gables, bevelled dentil molding, voussoirs and keystones

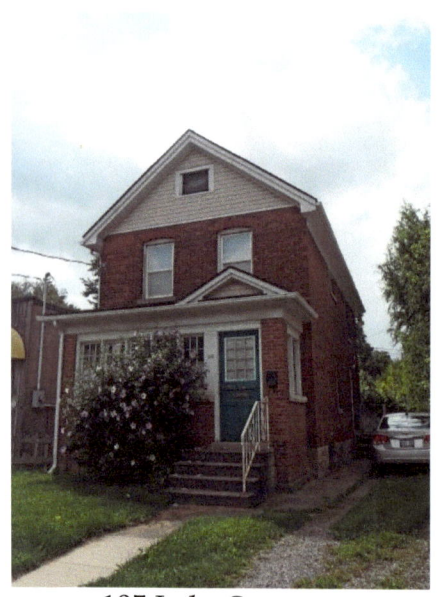

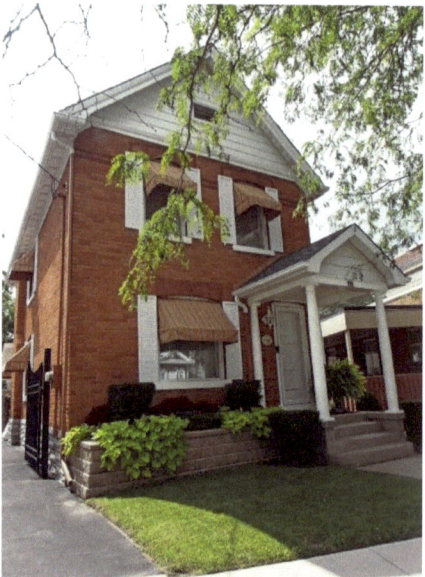

105 Lake Street
Edwardian, pediment

111 Lake Street
Edwardian

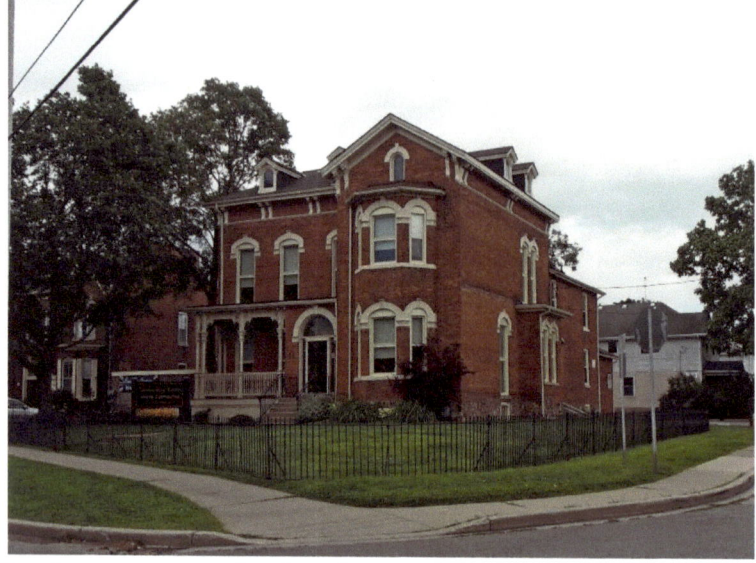

#72 – dormers, cornice brackets, string course, voussoirs and keystones, two-storey bay window, rectangular bay window on side, bric-a-brac on veranda, sidelights and transom

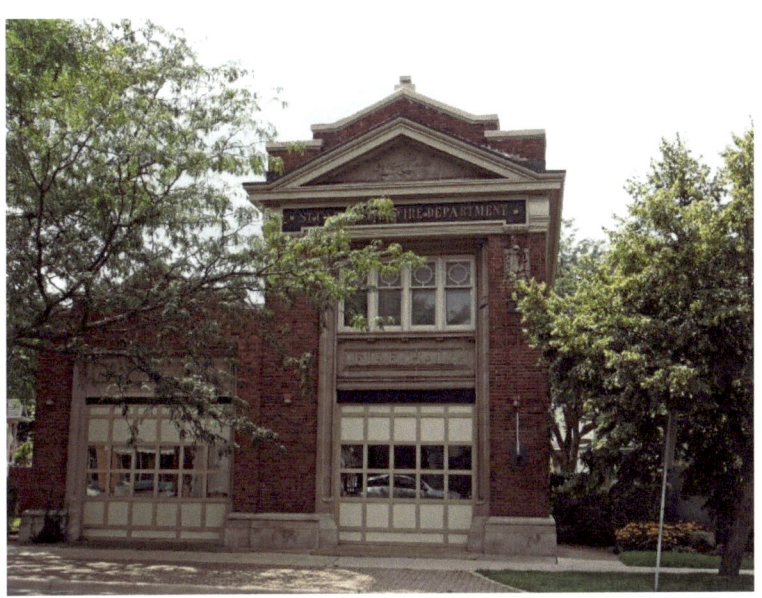

113 Lake Street – The former Grantham Fire Hall was constructed of steel and masonry in the Neo-Tudor style. The traditional red brick façade is laid in Flemish bond pattern; there is an elaborate decorative painted wood cornice and frieze. Decorative, rare circle muntin bars are in second floor windows. A stone carving set in entablature over the main door shows a fire carriage being pulled by horses, and stone plaques set in masonry show the firefighting crest. The building was built to accommodate a horse drawn hose wagon but by 1920 a four cylinder Reo fire truck was being used.

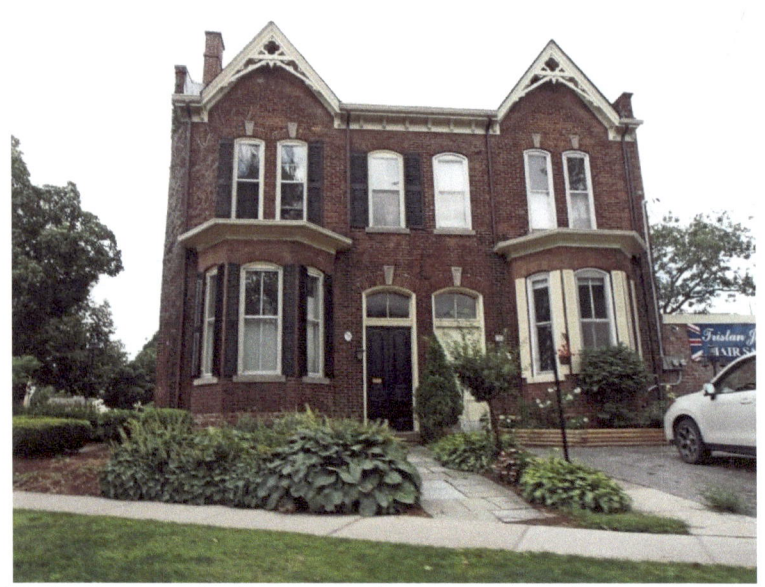

76 Lake Street – Italianate style, verge board trim on gables, voussoirs and keystones, bay windows, transom windows

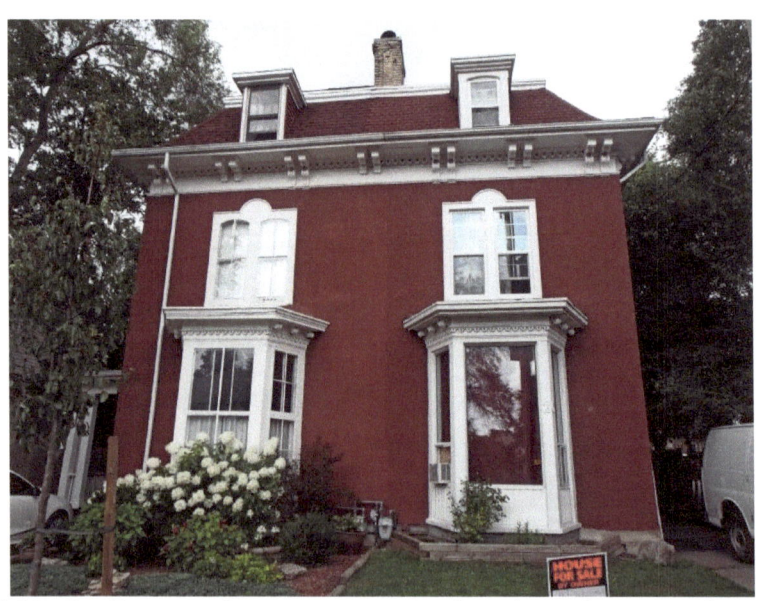

26 Lake Street – dormers, cornice brackets, bay windows

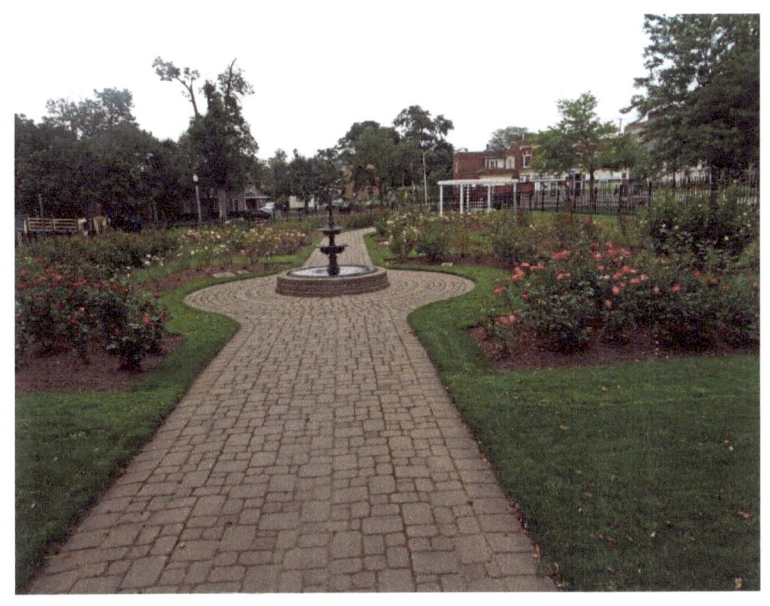

Montebello Park Rose garden

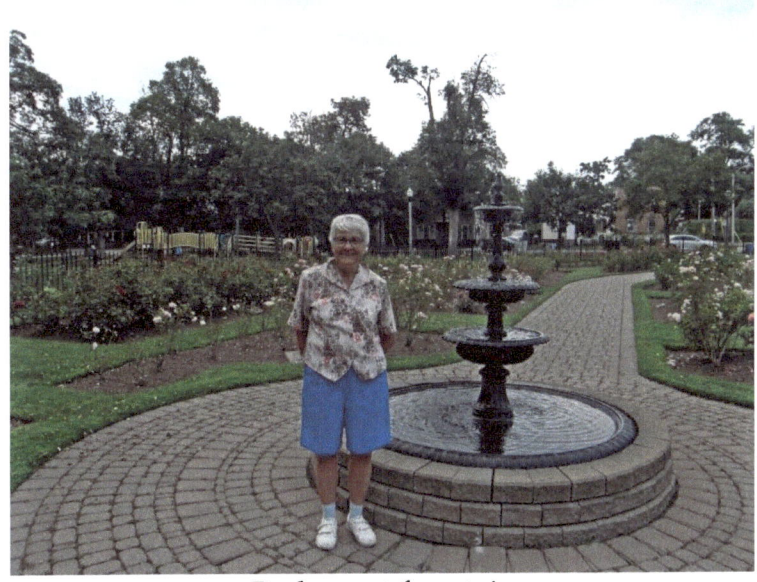

Barbara at fountain

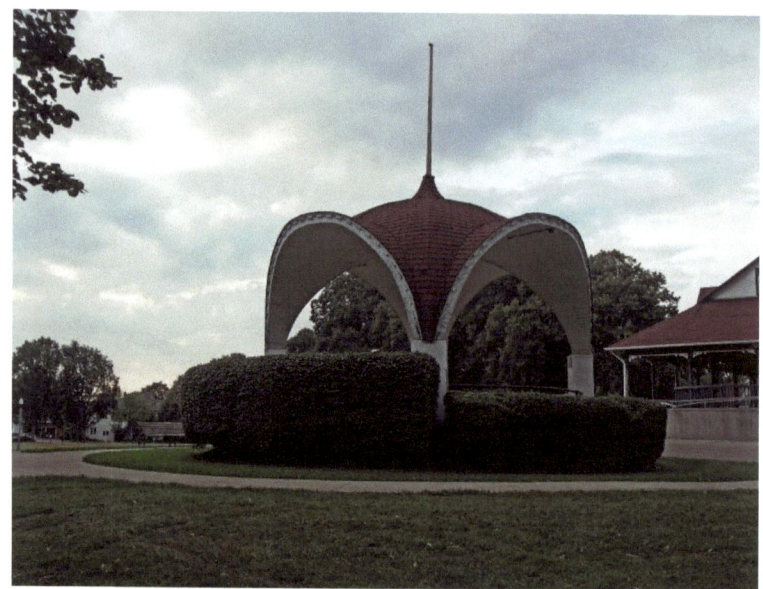

The T. Roy Adams Bandshell was named in honour of a former mayor whose love of people and music enriched St. Catharines for many years.

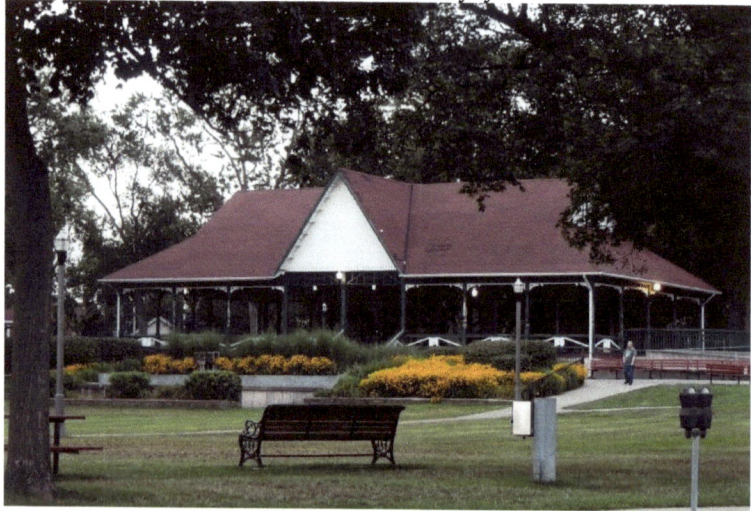

The Walter Ostanek Pavilion was dedicated on September 23, 2007 to celebrate 50 years of Canada's Polka King. In 1957 Ostanek formed his own band and in 1963 they recorded their first of more than 50 albums.

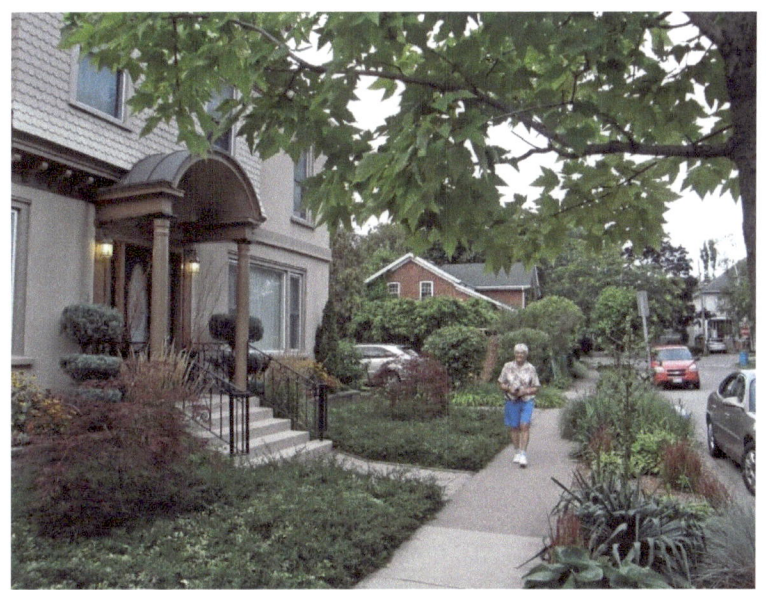
Walking down Midland Street

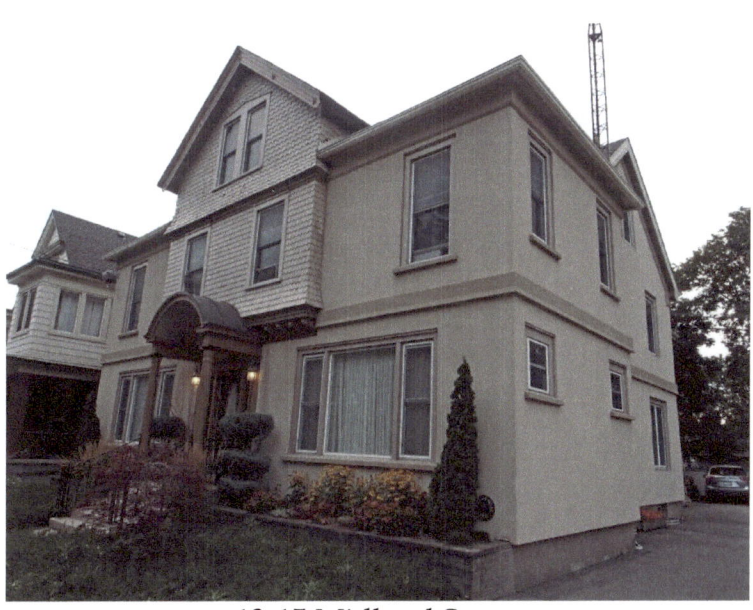
13-15 Midland Street

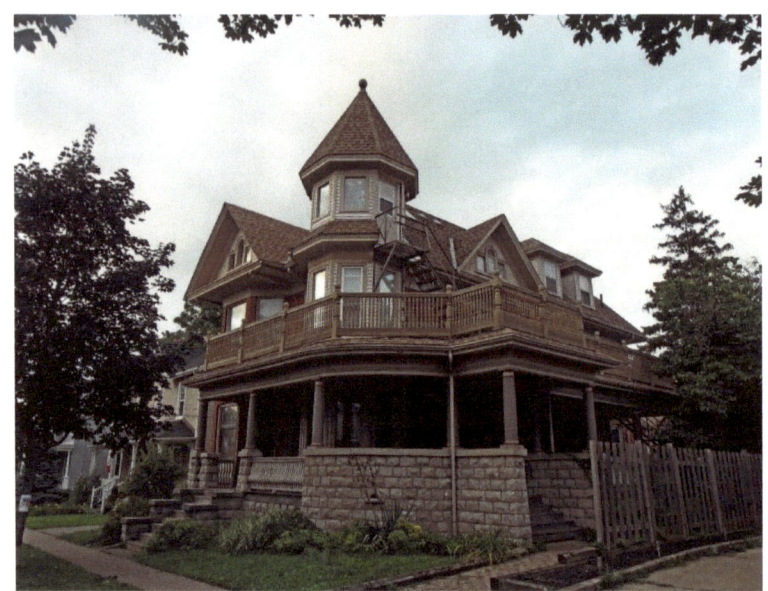

1 Montebello Place – Queen Anne style – varied roofline, turret, wraparound veranda on two levels, Palladian windows in gables, dormers

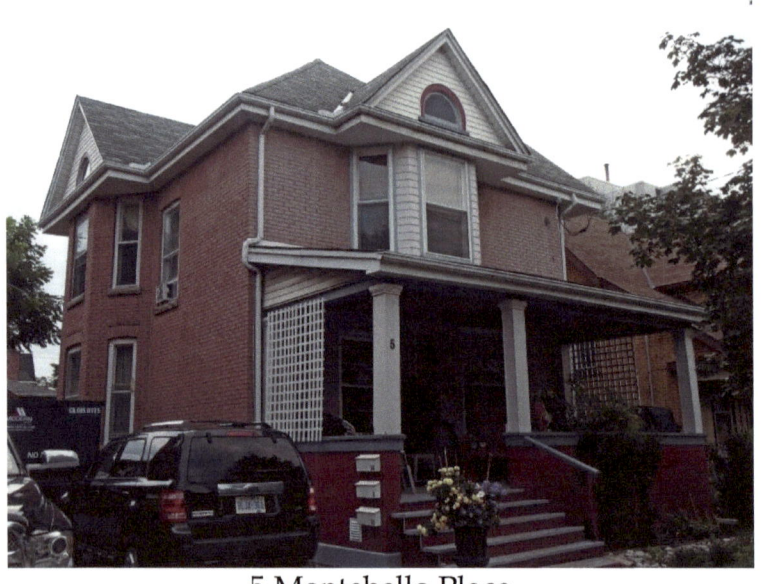

5 Montebello Place

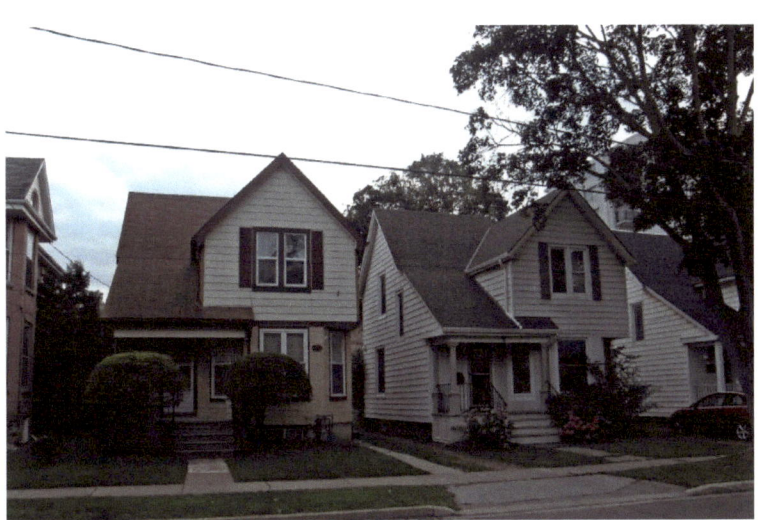

7 and 9 Montebello Place

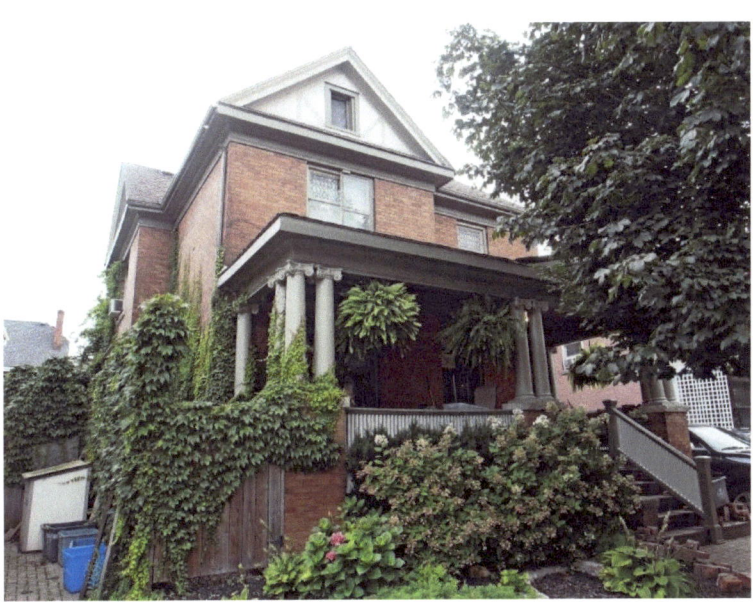

8 Montebello Place – Ionic capitals

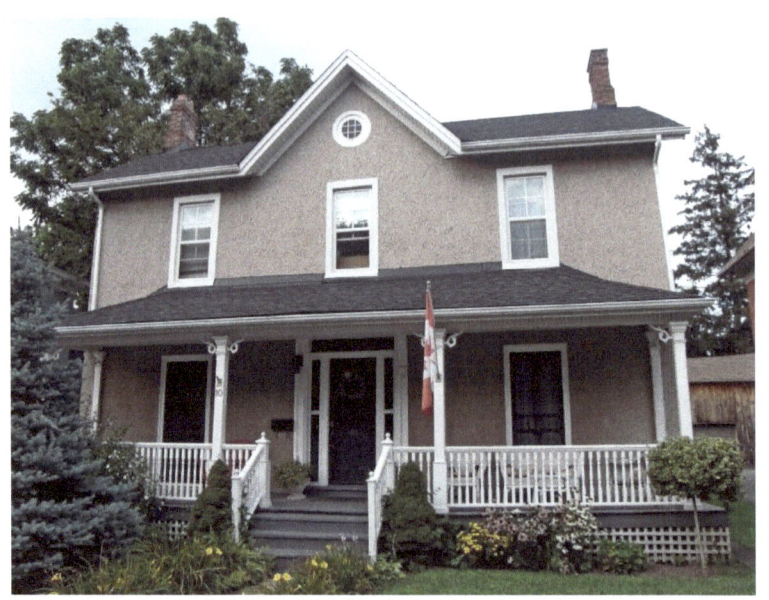

10 Montebello Place - Gothic

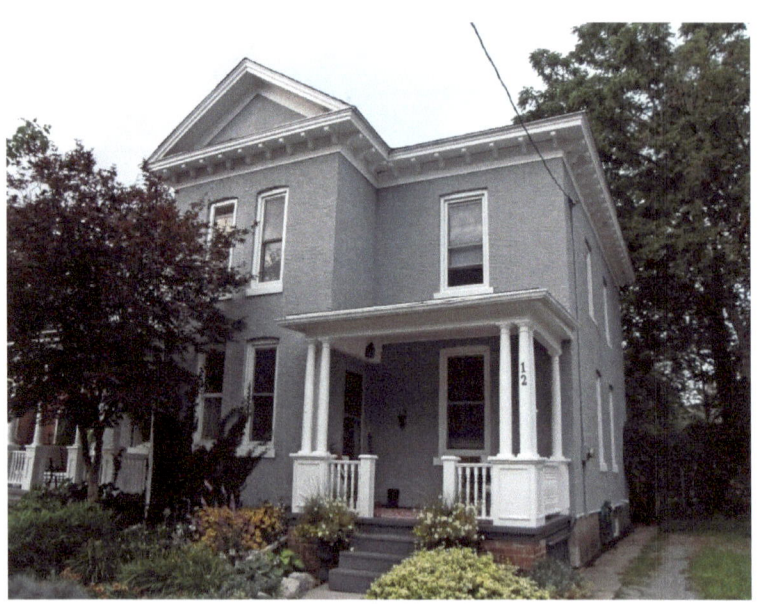

12 Montebello Place

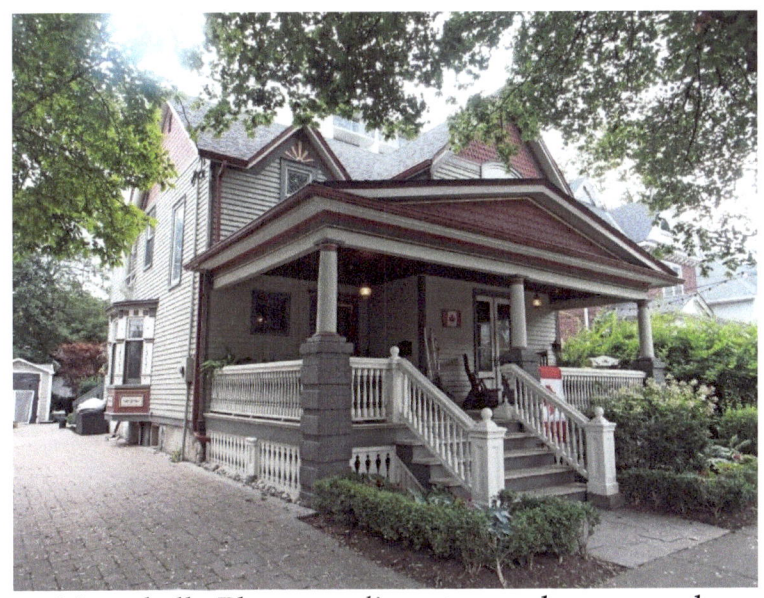

Montebello Place – pediment over deep veranda

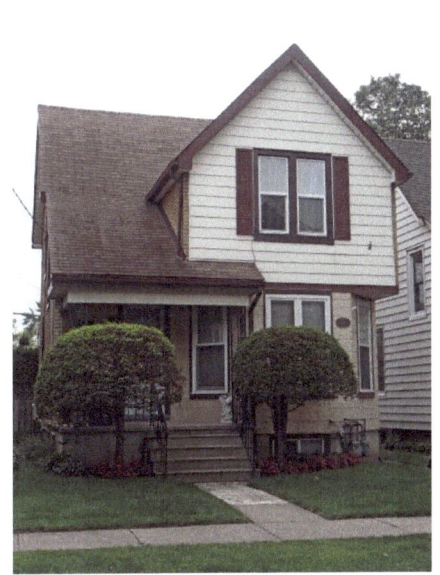

Montebello Place
c. 1900

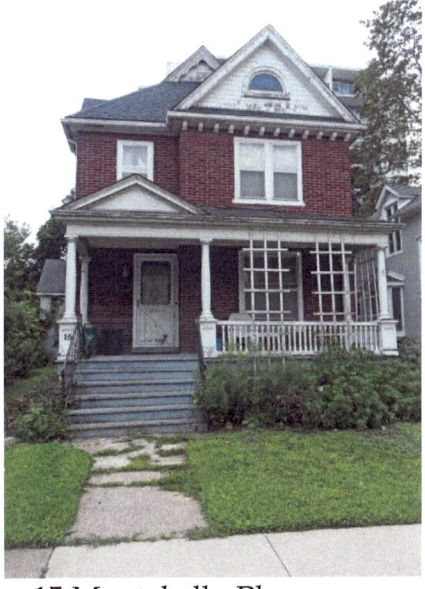

15 Montebello Place
pediment

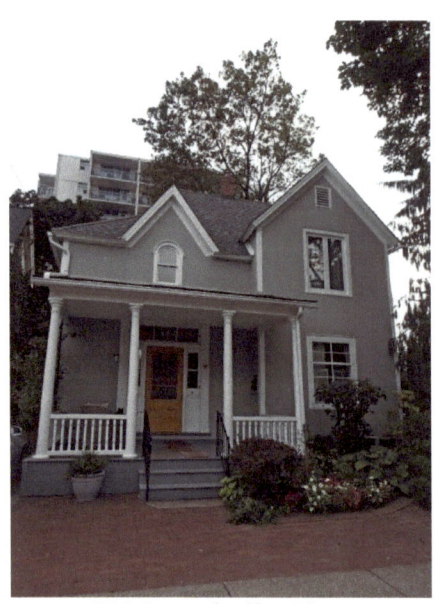

17 Montebello Place

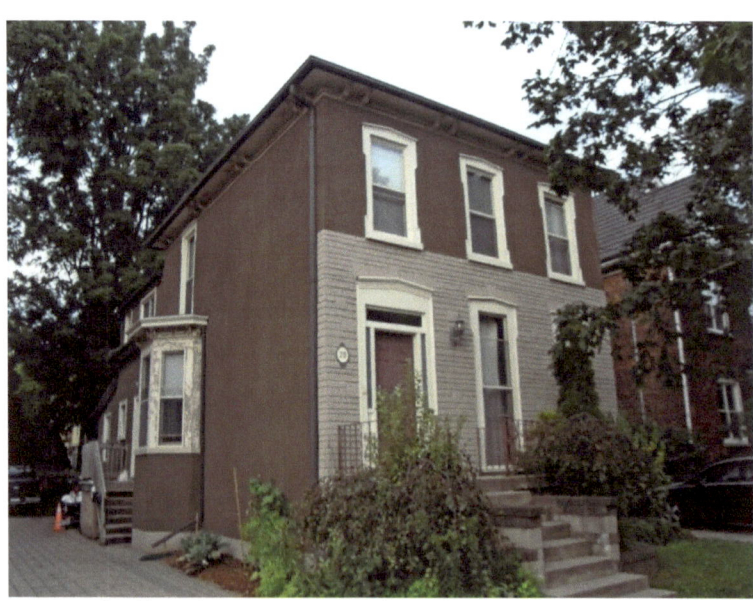

20 Montebello Place - cornice brackets, bay window on side

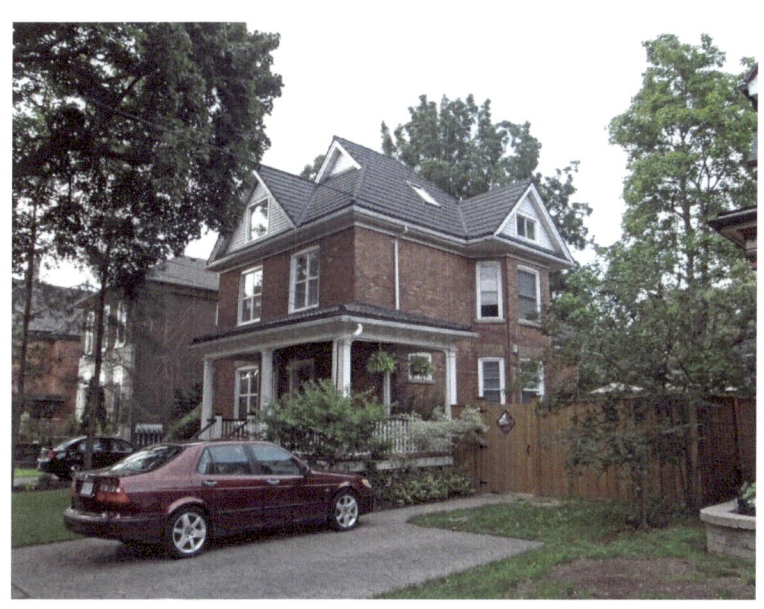

18 Montebello Place

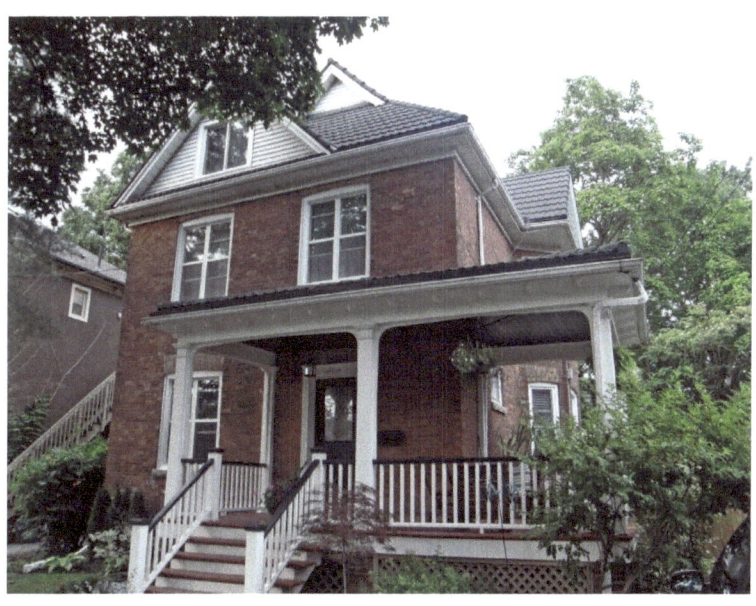

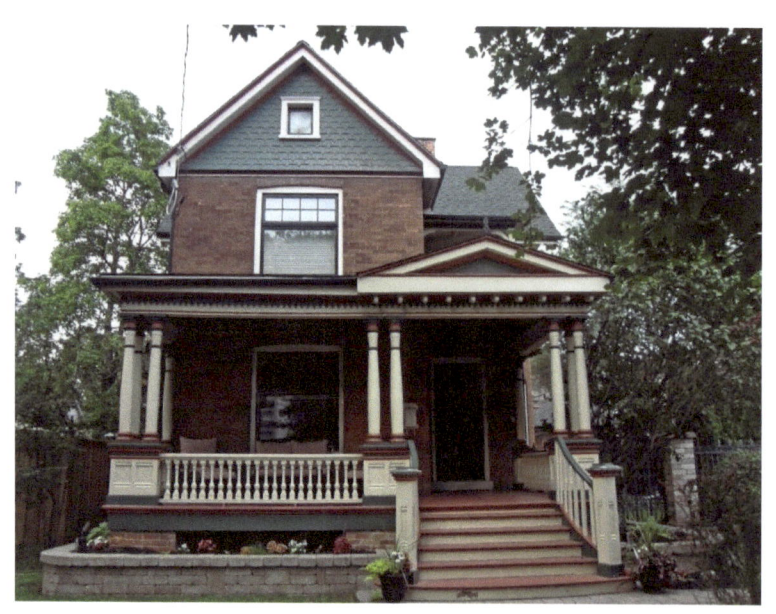

Montebello Place - pediment

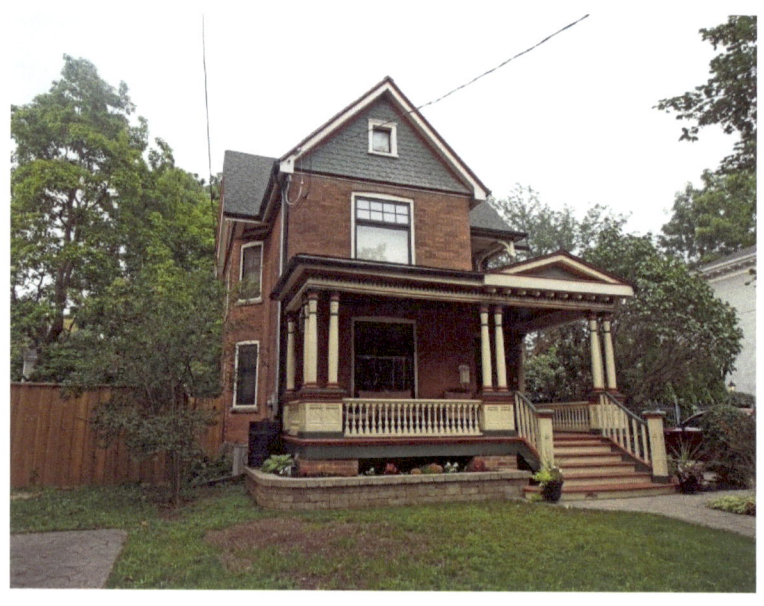

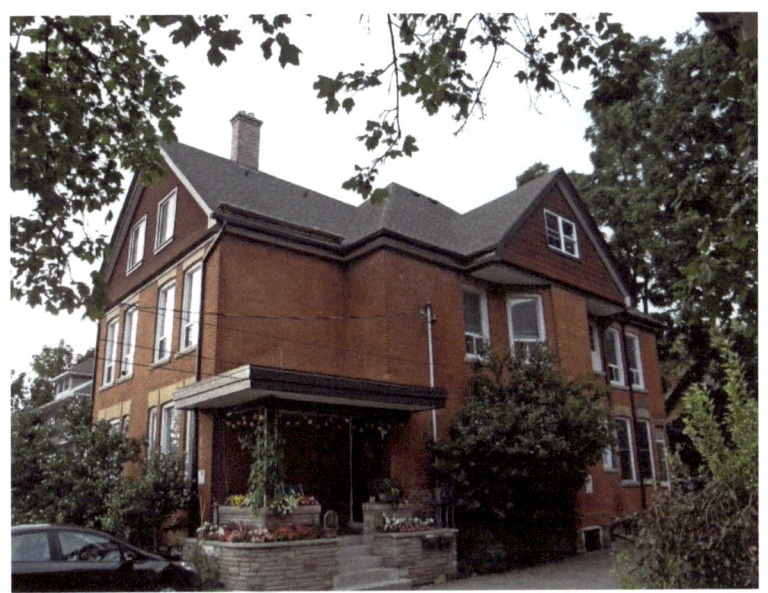

Montebello Place

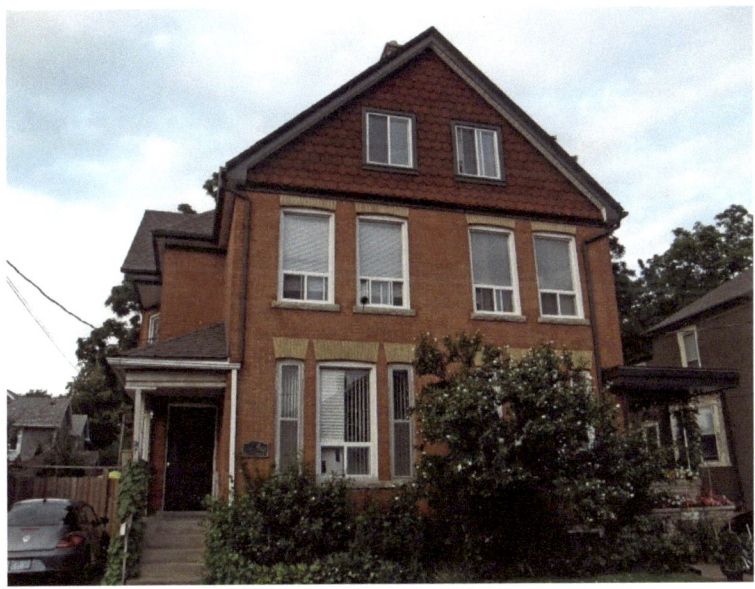

24 Montebello Place

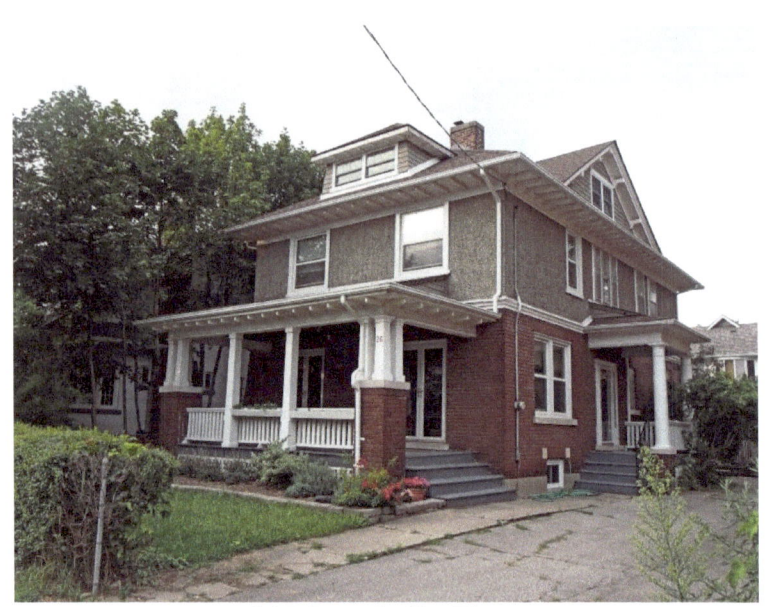

26 Montebello Place

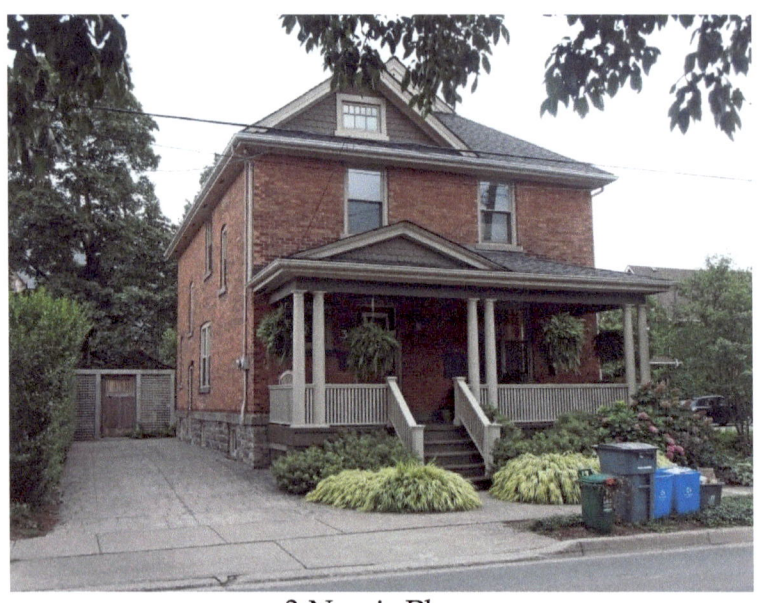

3 Norris Place

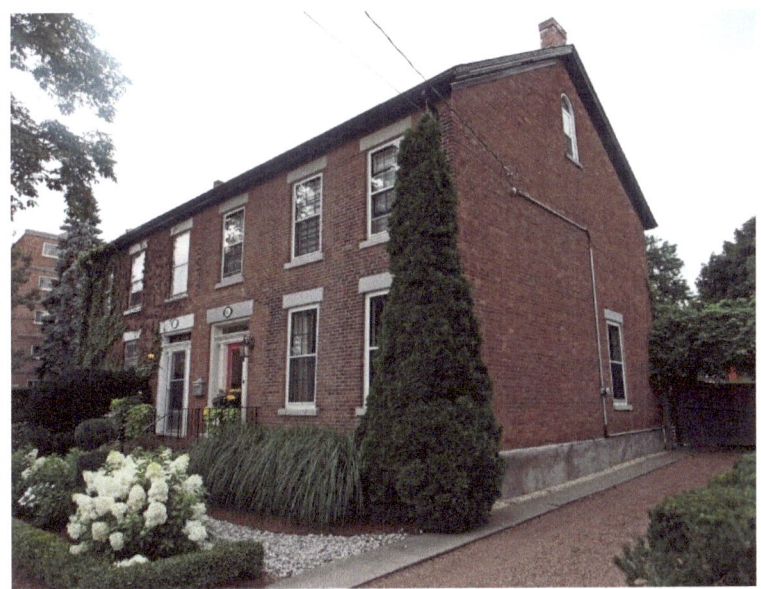

6-8 Norris Place

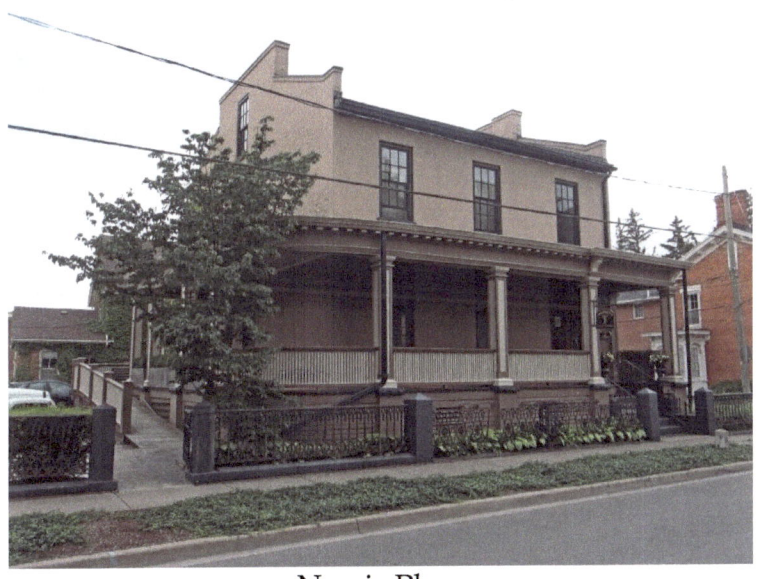

Norris Place

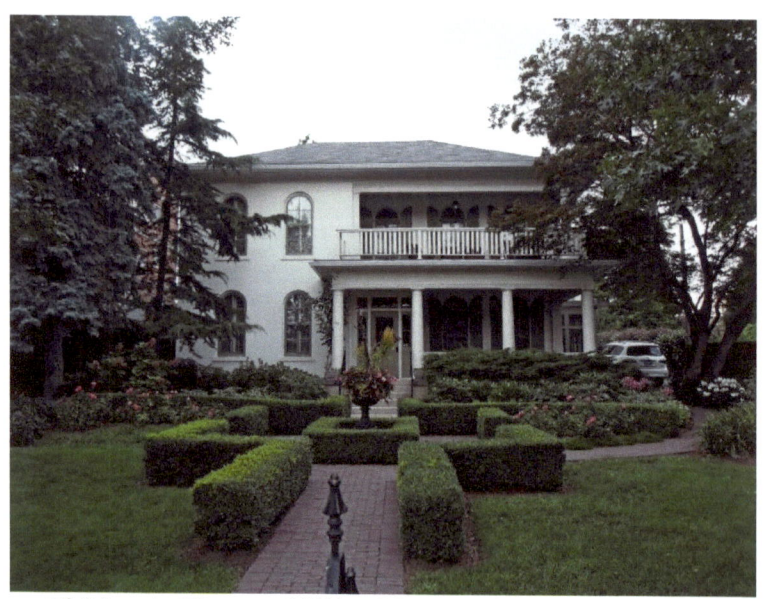

10 Norris Place – 1874 – Norris Place in St. Catharines, Ontario is named after Captain James Norris who was a sea captain, businessman, Mayor of St Catharines and Member of Parliament.

James Norris, one of the successful business men and leading manufacturers of St. Catharines, was born in Argyleshire, Scotland, in February 1820. At age fourteen, immigrated with his family to Upper Canada. When he was nineteen or twenty years of age, he came to St. Catharines, sailing on the lakes and Welland Canal in the season of navigation.

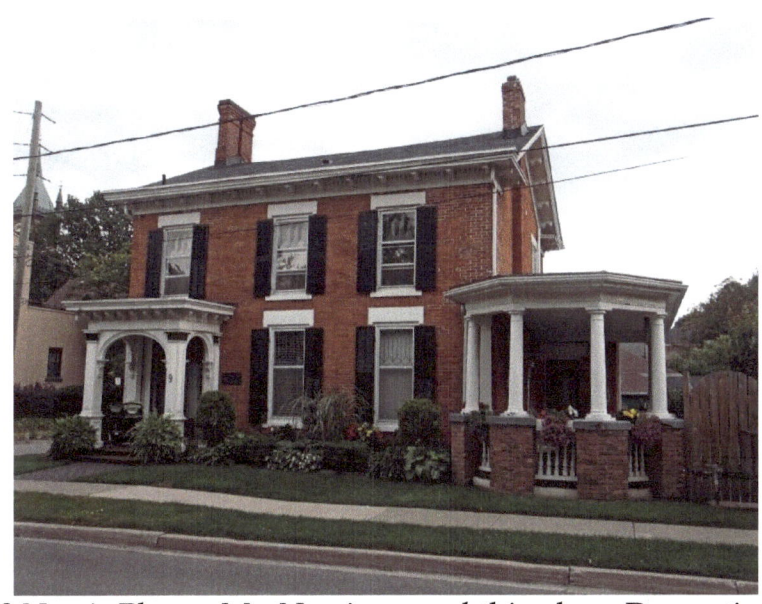

9 Norris Place – Mr. Norris owned this place. Decorative entrance, octagonal veranda

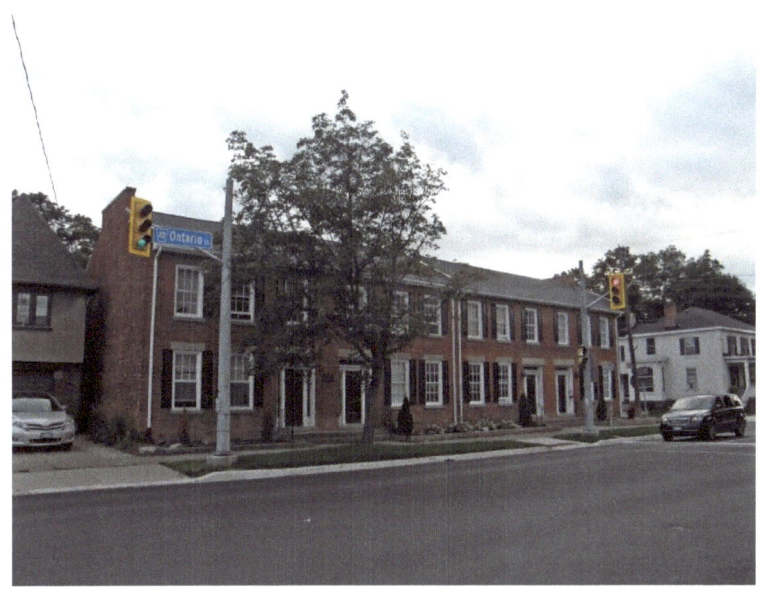

Ontario Street

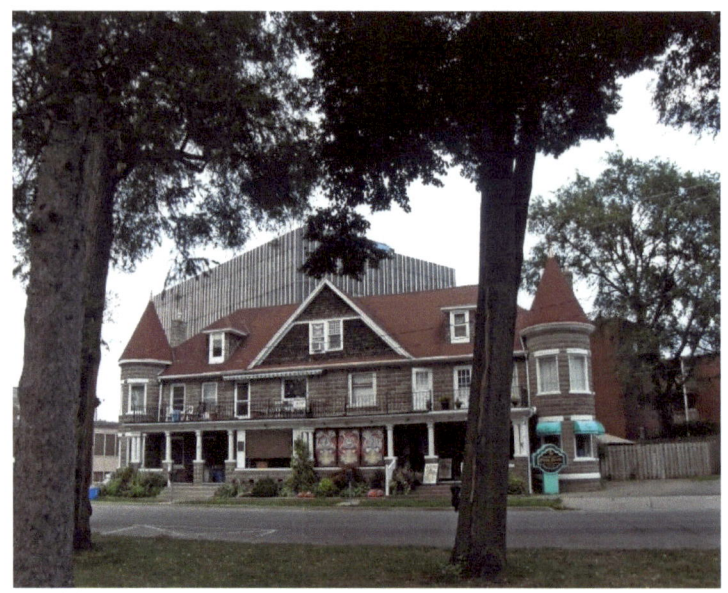

Gable in centre, dormers, and turrets on either end

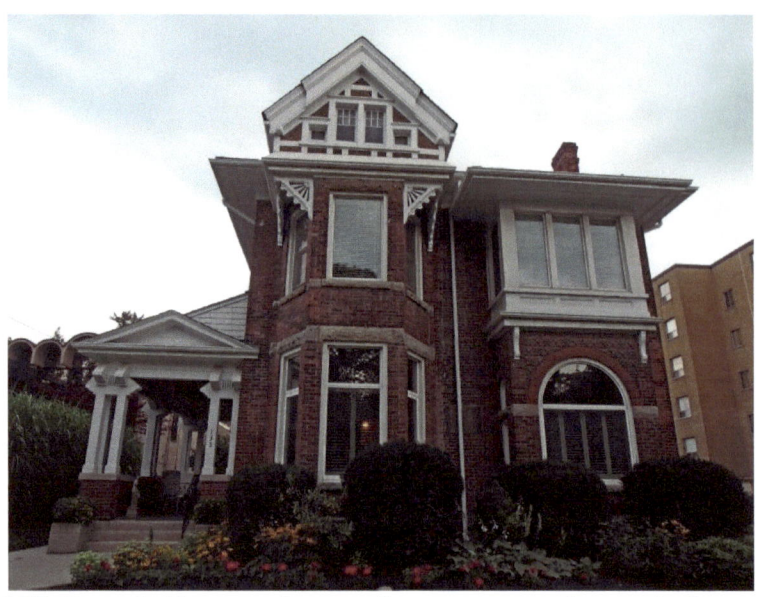

135 Ontario Street – fretwork, two storey bay windows, pediment

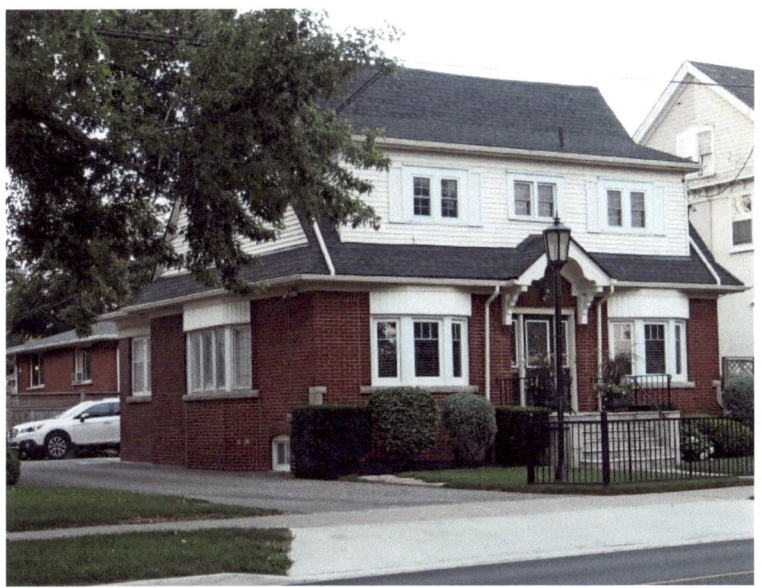

Shed dormer, bay windows

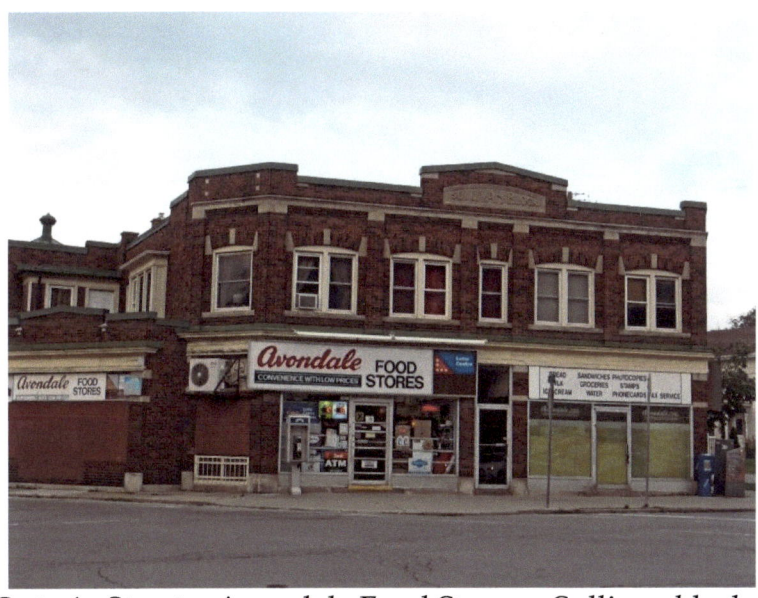

Ontario Street – Avondale Food Stores – Sullivan block – parapet, stone and brick voussoirs

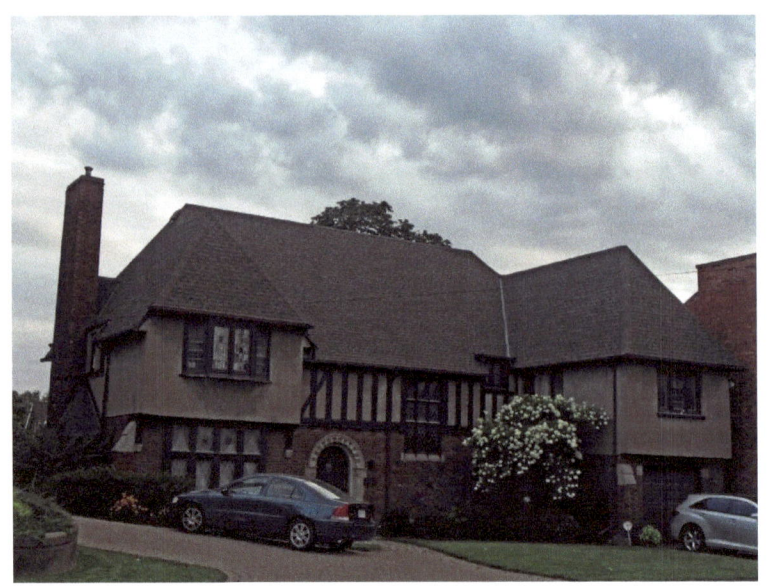

103 Ontario Street

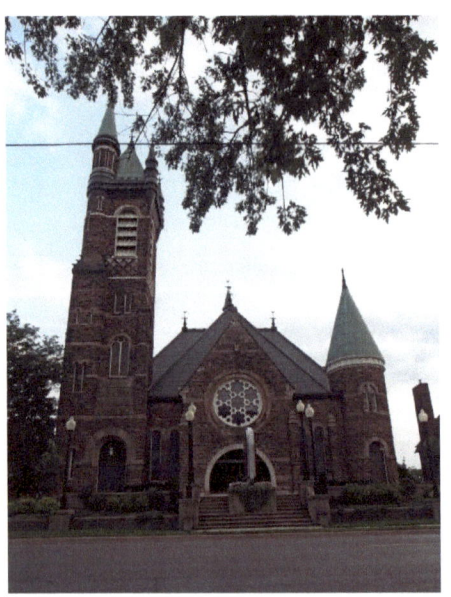

99 Ontario Street – St. Thomas Church – 1879 - Richardson Romanesque style with four storey tower and a two storey tower, rose window

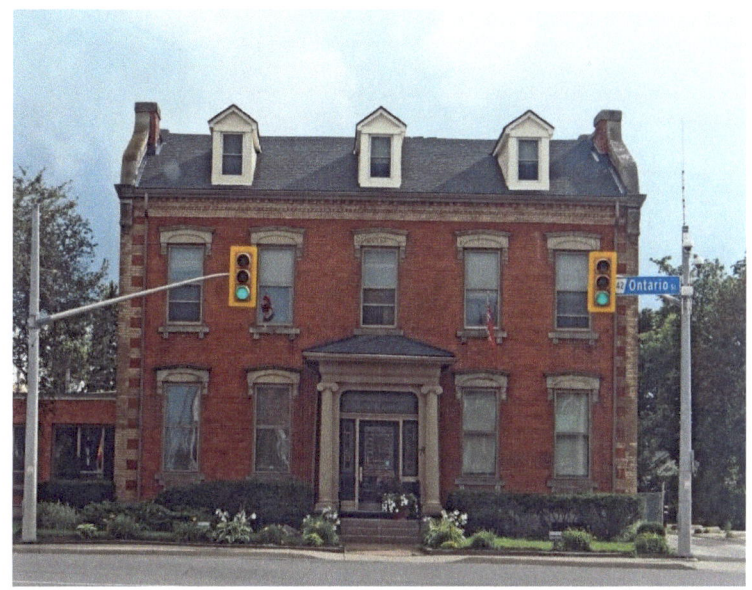

77 Ontario Street – dormers, corner quoins, pillared entrance with Ionic capitals

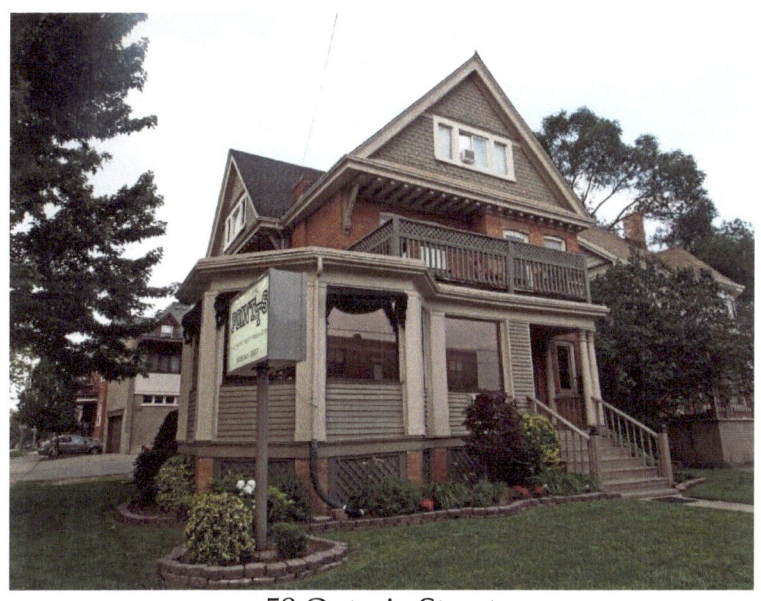

58 Ontario Street

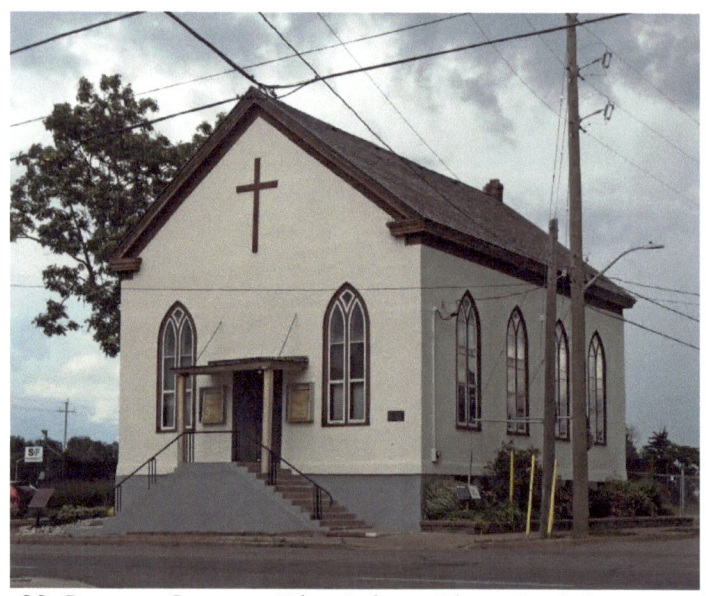

92 Geneva Street – The Salem Chapel of the British Missionary Episcopal Church was the first Black church in St. Catharines. In 1793 the "Upper Canada Act Against Slavery" was passed which allowed Blacks aged 25 years and older freedom from slavery in Canada. This created a safe haven for African American runaway slaves and made Canada the destination for many who fled. Hundreds of escaped slaves settled in St. Catharines and created a vibrant Black community.

The freedom seekers who settled here constructed this church and dedicated it in 1855. St. Catharines played an important role in the Underground Railroad movement. It was the chief terminal of Harriet Tubman's activities in Canada. Harriet Tubman, nicknamed "Black Moses" was a brave freedom fighter instrumental in freeing hundreds of slaves using the Underground Railroad system.

When she arrived in 1851 with eleven freedom seekers, she met Reverend Hiram Wilson at the American Methodist Episcopal Church, which became her place of worship. For the next seven years, Harriet continued to bring all slaves who dared to escape to St. Catharines.

When Harriet arrived in St. Catharines, the church was known as "Bethel Chapel" AME. It was a small log building constructed by African-American freedom seekers. In 1853, it was decided that a larger church was needed to assist the growing Methodist congregation that arrived via the Underground Railroad. The larger church was completed in 1855.

In 1855, it was decided that the AME Churches in Canada would change their name to establish their own distinct identity. This church was named the British Methodist Episcopal (BME) Church. The British Crown of England granted permission to use the word British in their title.

Architectural Terms

Battlement: A design for a parapet that has alternating solid parts and openings, originally used for defense, but later used as a decorative motif. Example: 81 Lake Street, Page 33	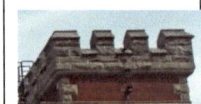
Bay Window: A window that projects out from a wall, in a semicircular, rectangular, or polygonal design. Used frequently in Gothic and Victorian designs. Example: 26 Lake Street, Page 38	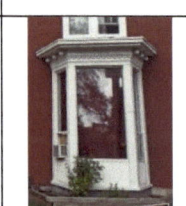
Brackets: a decorative or weight-bearing structural element which forms a right angle with one side against a wall and the other under a projecting surface such as an eave or roof. Example: #72, Page 36	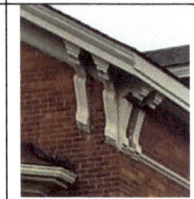
Buttress: a masonry structure built against or projecting from a wall which serves to support or reinforce the wall. In Canadian architecture, they are sometimes used for decoration. Example: 53 Church Street, Page 10	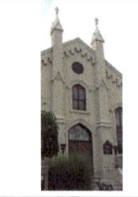
Capital: The uppermost finish or decoration on a column. An Ionic column has a small base, a thin elegant shaft, and a capital composed of volutes which are carved whirls or twists that take the form of a scroll. Example: 8 Montebello Place, Page 43	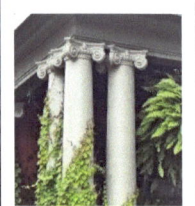
Cornice: originally the wooden overhang of the roof. With the use of stone, brick, iron and steel, the cornice is any horizontal moulded projection at the top of a building. They can be very decorative. Example: 183 King Street, Page 30	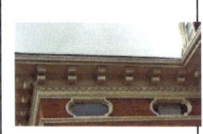

Cupola: A domed or curved roof rising from a building as a decorative element. Example: 101 King Street, Page 24	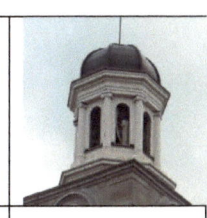
Dentil Moulding: an even series of rectangles used as ornamental decoration in cornices. Example: 127-129 Lake Street, Page 35	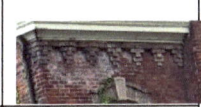
Dormer: (French for "sleep") a gable end window that pierces through the plane of a sloping roof surface to create usable space in the top floor or attic of a building by adding headroom. Example: 171 King Street, Page 28	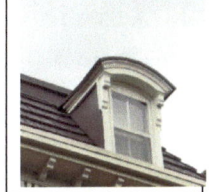
Entrance: The entrance encompasses the doorway and the inner vestibule or, in residential architecture, the covered porch. Example: 9 Norris Place, Page 53	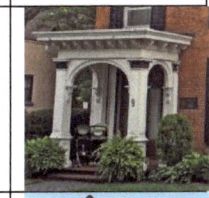
Gable: the triangular portion of a wall between the edges of a sloping roof. Example: 214 King Street, Page 31	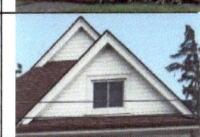
Hipped Roof: a roof where all sides slope downwards to the walls with no gables. Example: 97 Church Street, Page 16	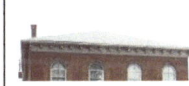
Keystones and Voussoirs: a voussoir is a wedge-shaped element used in building an arch. A keystone is the central stone that locks all the stones into position, allowing the arch to bear weight. A keystone is often enlarged and embellished. Example: 76 Lake Street, Page 38	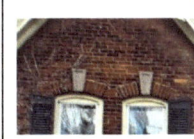

Lancet Window: a tall, narrow window with a pointed arch at its top. Example: 53 Church Street, Page 10	
Mansard Roof: This style was popularized by Francois Mansart (1598-1666), an accomplished architect of the French Baroque period and especially fashionable during the Second French Empire (1852-1870). This roof is almost flat on the top section, with two slopes on each of its sides with the lower slope at a steeper angle than the upper, and has dormer windows. Example: 106-108 Church Street, Page 18	
Palladian Window: a large window that is divided into three sections with the centre section larger than the two side sections and usually arched. Example: 107 Church Street, Page 16	
Parapet: low wall around the edge of a roof. Example: 14 James Street, Page 20	
Pediment: a triangular section above the door or portico, usually supported by columns. The inside of the triangle is called the tympanum. Example: 113 Lake Street, Page 37	
Quoin: masonry blocks at the corner of a wall, often a decorative feature, usually larger or of a different colour than the rest of the wall. Example: 77 Ontario Street, Page 57	

Rose Window: a circular window with ornamental tracery radiating from the centre. Example: 99 Ontario Street, Page 56	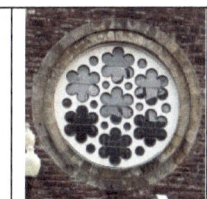
Sidelight: a vertical window that flanks a door, and is often used to emphasize the importance of a primary entrance. **Transom Window:** the light above the doorway, also called a fanlight. Example: 31 Church Street, Page 10	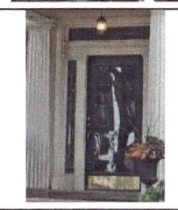
Tower: A circular, square, or octagonal vertical structure higher than the surrounding structure that is usually part of an existing building and is created either for extra defense or for a specific purpose such as a clock or a bell tower. Example: 164 King Street, Page 27	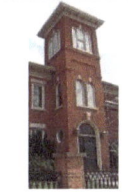
Turret: a small tower that projects from the wall of a building. Example: 1 Montebello Place, Page 42	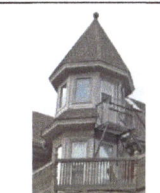
Verge board and Finial: also called bargeboards – hang from the projecting end of a roof and are often elaborately carved and ornamented. **Finial:** ornament added to the top of a gable, pinnacle, canopy or spire – a Gothic element. Example: 26-30 Church Street, Page 9	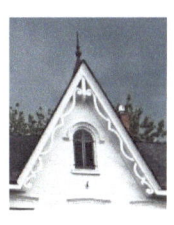

Window Hood: A **hood** is the piece found above window openings, usually of an ornate design, and covers the top third of the opening. Hoods are commonly placed above arched or curved openings on both windows and doors.

Example: 106-108 Church Street, Page 18

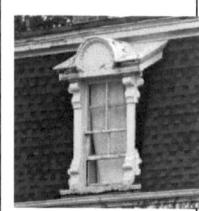

Building Styles

Art Deco, 1910-1940 - The Art Deco Style was developed for the French luxury market after World War I. Art Deco left its mark on everything from lamps and foot stools to purses and hair combs. The style was adopted in Ontario by wealthy and very fashionable patrons who wanted Art Deco detailing to make their buildings look lavish and exotic. Example: 145 King Street, Page 26	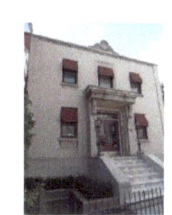
Classical Revival, 1820-1860 – This style was an analytical, scientific, and dogmatic revival based on intensive studies of Greek and Roman buildings, concerned with the application of Greek plans and proportions to civic buildings. Schools, libraries, government offices, and most other civic buildings were built in the Classical Revival style. The white columned porches of the Classical Revival domestic buildings are identified with the mansions of wealthy land owners in Canada. Example: Oille Fountain, Page 25	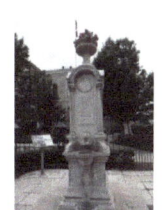

Edwardian, 1900-1930 – This style bridges the ornate and elaborate styles of the Victorian era and the simplified styles of the 20th century. Edwardian Classicism provided simple, balanced facades, simple rooflines, dormer windows, large front porches, and smooth brick surfaces. Voussoirs and keystones are used sparingly and are understated. Finials and cresting are absent. Cornice brackets and braces are block-like and openings have flat arches or plain stone lintels. Example: 105 Lake Street, Page 36	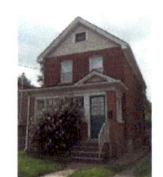
Georgian, before 1860 – This style began with the British King Georges in the 18th century. These buildings have balanced facades around a central door, medium-pitched gable roofs, and small paned windows. Example: 101 King Street, Page 24	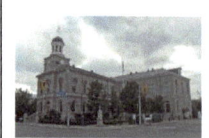
Gothic Revival, 1830-1890 – These decorative buildings have sharply-pitched gables with highly detailed verge boards, pointed-arch window openings, and dichromatic brickwork. It is a common style in Ontario. Example: 26-30 Church Street, Page 9	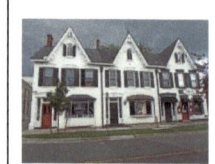

Italianate, 1850-1900 – A two story rectangular building with a mild hip roof, a projecting frontispiece, and generous eaves with ornate cornice brackets was the basis of the style; often there are large sash windows, quoins, ornate detailing on the windows, belvederes and wraparound verandahs. Italianate commercial buildings often have cast iron cresting and elegant window surrounds. Example: 76 Lake Street, Page 38	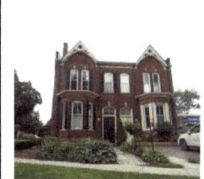
Queen Anne, 1885-1900 – This style is distinguished by an irregular outline featuring a combination of an offset tower, broad gables, projecting two-storey bays, verandahs, multi-sloped roofs, and tall, decorative chimneys. A mixture of brick and wood is common. Windows often have one large single-paned bottom sash and small panes in the upper sash. Example: 1 Montebello Place, Page 42	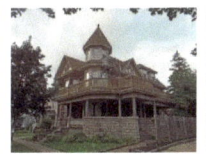

Richardsonian Romanesque Revival, 1870-1910 – is a style of Romanesque Revival architecture which incorporates 11th and 12th century southern French, Spanish and Italian Romanesque characteristics. It emphasizes clear, strong picturesque massing, round-headed Romanesque arches which often spring from clusters of short squat columns, recessed entrances, richly varied rustication, blank stretches of walls contrasting with bands of windows, and cylindrical towers with conical caps embedded in the walls. Example: 99 Ontario Street, Page 56	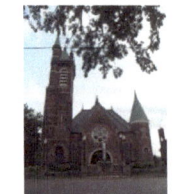
Second Empire, 1860-1880 – The mansard roof is the most noteworthy feature of this style and is evidence of the French origins. Projecting central towers and one or two-storey bays can also be present. Example: 106-108 Church Street, Page 18	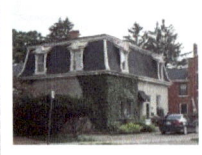
Tudor Revival – exposed timbers with stucco infill, multi-paned windows. Example: 113 Lake Street, Page 37	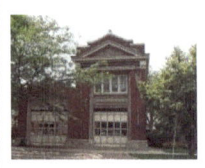

www.ingramcontent.com/pod-product-compliance
Lightning Source LLC
Chambersburg PA
CBHW040232220526
45473CB00001B/215